THE ART OF BA GUA ZHANG

MEDITATION • HEALTH • SELF-DEFENSE • EXERCISE • LONGEVITY • MOTION SCIENCE • PHILOSOPHY OF LIVING

TOM BISIO

The Art of Ba Gua Zhang: Meditation * Health * Self-Defense * Exercise * Longevity * Motion Science * Philosophy of Living
All Rights Reserved.
Copyright © 2016
By Tom Bisio v2.0

Outskirts Press, Inc.
http://www.outskirtspress.com

ISBN: 978-1-4787-7744-1

Outskirts Press and the "OP" logo are trademarks belonging to Outskirts Press, Inc.

PRINTED IN THE UNITED STATES OF AMERICA

Disclaimer

The author and publisher of this book **are not responsible in any manner** for any injury or illness, which may result from following the instructions or performing the exercises contained within the book.

The activities described in this book, physical or otherwise, may be too strenuous or dangerous for a given individual.

Before embarking on **any** of the physical activities described in this book, the reader should consult his or her physician for advice regarding their individual suitability for performing such activity.

Any health benefits attributed to these movements and exercises, whether mentioned or inferred, are not advocated or promised by the author or publisher. Any health benefits, and the efficacy of the movements and techniques, whether mentioned or inferred, are those typically attributed to these movements and exercises in traditional Chinese culture. We neither endorse nor advocate these benefits and opinions, nor do we vouch for their veracity. They are presented for educational and historical purposes only.

Contents

Introduction

1. What is Ba Gua Zhang?   1

2. Ba Gua Zhang and the *Yi Jing*   9

3. Ba Gua Zhang and Daoism   21

4. Health Benefits of Ba Gua Zhang   27

5. Ba Gua Zhang for Exercise and Physical Fitness   47

6. Who Can Practice Ba Gua Zhang?   53

7. What is an Internal Martial Art?   73

8. Ba Gua Zhang as Exercise & Physical Therapy   97

9. Ba Gua Zhang as a Martial Art   107

10. Ba Gua Zhang as a Psycho-Spiritual Path   145

11. Overview of the Ba Gua Zhang Curriculum   155

Appendix: Beijing Ba Gua Health Study   158

INTRODUCTION

Ba Gua Zhang (Eight Diagram Palm) has its origins in China's past, but it is an art that transcends cultural and language barriers. Its unique theory and practice make Ba Gua Zhang suitable for many people and many purposes. Although a product of China's martial history and culture, Ba Gua Zhang has broad application to many aspects of human life that cross cultural boundaries: self-defense, building health, promoting longevity, exercise and fitness, motion science and cultivation of mind, body and spirit. The connection Ba Gua Zhang with the *Yi Jing* (Book of Changes), and its roots in Daoist natural science, instill in the practitioner a practical philosophy of living, while simultaneously providing a path for spiritual growth and transformation.

In China, martial arts and self-cultivation have gone hand-in-hand for centuries, allowing arts like Ba Gua Zhang to transcend the realm of sport, exercise and self-defense and achieve recognition as vehicles for character development, promoting longevity and enhancing life. Following in this tradition, the founder of Ba Gua Zhang is reputed to have combined the most effective martial arts, meditation, and self-cultivation methods with Chinese Medicine and Daoist internal alchemy in order to create this art.

Philosophy, life-cultivation and self-defense are seamlessly combined into Ba Gua Zhang's theories and training methods. Both the inside and outside of a person are cultivated simultaneously. The foundational training, circular walking, and changing palms strengthen muscles, tendons, sinews and bones, while simultaneously harmonizing the functions of the internal organs, stimulating the brain and nervous system, unblocking the meridians and fostering the development of an indomitable spirit.

The practice of Ba Gua Zhang cultivates both one's life (*Ming*) and one's inner nature (*Xing*). Life cultivation refers to the aspects of the art relating to health science, longevity, movement, self-defense, and exercise. Inner nature refers to cultivation of the Heart-Mind, and Spirit (*Shen*) the aspects of Ba Gua Zhang that relate to meditation, philosophy and mental cultivation and spiritual growth. In Daoism this dual-cultivation is considered to be the most balanced and natural method of cultivating mind, body and spirit.

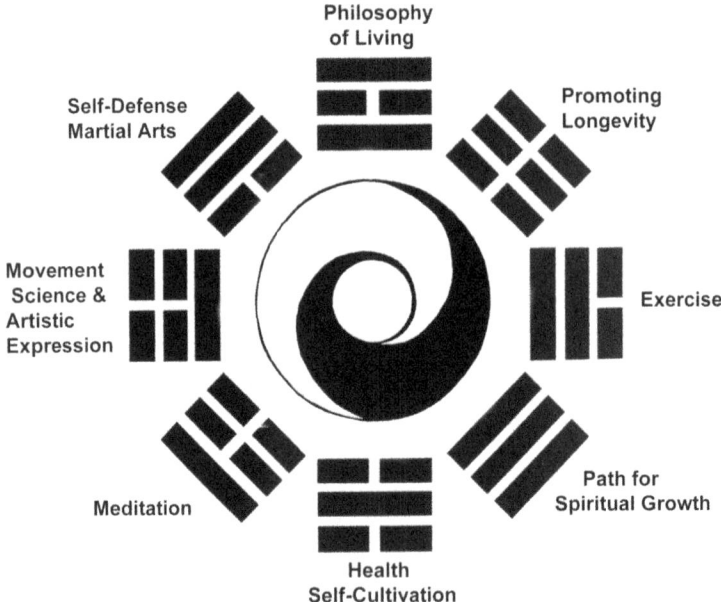

The Complete Art of Ba Gua Zhang

The inherent genius of the long tradition culminating in the art of Ba Gua Zhang is that all of these aspects of the art are integrated into an connected, organic whole. Practicing any one part of the art reinforces and enhances every other part. This generates an exponential potential for growth and development in each practitioner.

This book is an introduction to the many facets of Ba Gua Zhang. A good portion of the discussion is from my own perspective and experiences, the perspectives of my teachers, and the perspectives of the Ba Gua lineages I have followed and trained. There are other pother perspectives, other lineages and other teachers and their experiences are equally valid. So this is by no means a definitive discussion, yet at the same time much of what is discussed here does relate to most Ba Gua methods that are taught today.

In particular, circular walking is central to the practice of Ba Gua Zhang and to all styles of Ba Gua Zhang. Walking and turning, while cultivating the mind and the breath has many profound affects on the human body, mind and nervous system. Some of these are documented in the following pages, but many can only be understood through the practice itself.

WHAT IS BA GUA ZHANG?

Ba Gua Zhang is one of the *Nei Jia Chuan* "Inner School" or Internal Boxing Arts. There is some debate about which boxing arts qualify as being "internal." In China today most practitioners agree that the *Nei Jia* include the following five arts:

1. Tai Ji Quan (Great Ultimate Boxing)

2. Xing Yi Quan (Form Intention Boxing)

3. Ba Gua Zhang (Eight Diagram Palm)

4. Tong Bei Quan (White Ape Boxing)

5. Liu He Ba Fa (Six Harmonies & Eight Methods)

These five arts have in common certain principles that have come to be called "internal." This is in part due to the fact that they all stress correct body alignment, the development of "whole body power" and the unity of mind and body in every action. Another primary reason these arts are considered to be internal is due to their role as a type of internal alchemy that transforms *Qi*[1] into *Jing* (Essence). *Jing* in turn promotes the *Qi* and *Shen* (Spirit, Spiritual Energy or

---

[1] *Qi* has no simple definition. It can be understood as "energy" or "vital force." *Qi* also refers to breathing and respiration as well as fog, mists, and vapor – things that are perceptible, but intangible. In traditional Chinese medicine, *Qi* is the basis for the body's activity, but this activity is itself described as *Qi*. Proper or correct *Qi* maintains and renew the measured, orderly changes that comprise normal functioning of body processes. In the martial arts, *Qi* has a direct relationship with the power and movement generated through the muscles and bones in coordination with the breath.

Force). This transformative process serves to promote health and prolong life.

Characteristics of Ba Gua Zhang

Ba Gua Zhang or "Eight Diagram Palm" is a method of boxing that is characterized by footwork, evasive movement and constant change. The actions of the whole body are coordinated with the rotation of the waist and the walking action of the legs. These elements, when combined with relaxation and connection of mind and body, produce an explosive, coordinated power that comes from the unified action of the entire body and is not dependent on the relative strength of the external musculature.

Ba Gua's unique feature is its use of curved steps, and its practice of walking around a circle to train the mind and body and develop whole body power. The importance of circle walking is stressed in The Thirty-Six Songs, the oral instructions for correct training handed down through generations of teachers and students. For example:

This palm is quite different from others,

It is skillful to walk forward and raise the foot. (Song 12)

and

Curve the step and straighten the foot to extend forward.

Walk like pushing a millstone. (Song 3)

Although there are various theories about the origins of Ba Gua Zhang, Dong Hai Chuan is considered by most people to be the founder of Ba Gua. It is not known for certain what martial arts Dong studied in his youth, but there is evidence that he combined martial arts with Daoist meditation practices, which involved keeping the mind empty while walking in a circle. Dong was often quoted as saying, "training in martial arts is not as good as walking the circle."[2] Circle walking is considered one of the key exercises in Ba Gua, because it aids in evasion and counterattack and enables one to literally turn the opponent's corner in combat. In addition, circle walking calms the mind and trains both the spirit and internal energy.

The forms and techniques of Ba Gua are manifestations of the principles of whole body coordination or "internal connection." These internal connections are predicated on using circular and spiral forces to overcome external forces and attacks, and to concentrate and suddenly release the body's full power in combat. Furthermore, in both training and combat there is an emphasis on internal stillness while the body is in motion. Internally the mind and spirit are still and calm, while internally and externally the body constantly changes and transforms, able to create infinite techniques seamlessly linked together. That is why it is said that the basic skills of stepping and turning can create "1,000 changes and 10,000 transformations."

Transformation & Change

This idea of transformation can be expressed in many ways. Yin and Yang are concepts commonly used in any discussion of Ba Gua Zhang. In part, this arises from the connection of Ba Gua Zhang to the *Yi Jing* (Book of Changes). Combat can be a changing, unpredictable situation. Therefore Ba Gua emphasizes continuous movement, countering and re-countering, and dynamic states of change and transformation in accordance with the changing circumstances. These ideas are often described by using the juxtaposition of opposites: "stillness within motion", "stand like a nail and move like the wind", and

---

[2] *The Origins of Pa Kua Chang Part 3*, by Dan Miller and Kang Ge Wu (Pa Kua Chang Journal Vol. 3, No. 4 May/June 1993) p. 25-9.

"firmness and gentleness in mutual assistance." Another image used by Ba Gua practitioners is that one should "walk like a dragon, turn like a monkey and change like an eagle," varying the shape, spirit and dynamics of one's movements. Francois Jullien's description of the dragon motif in Chinese culture is a beautiful metaphor for this idea of constant change and could easily serve as description of Ba Gua Zhang in action:

> *The body of the dragon concentrates energy in its sinuous curves, and coils and uncoils to move along more quickly. It is a symbol with all the potential with which form can be charged, a potential that never ceases to be actualized. The dragon now lurks in watery depths, now streaks aloft to the highest heavens, and its very gait is a continuous undulation. It presents an image of energy constantly recharged through oscillation from one pole to the other.*[3]

Although Ba Gua Zhang literally means "Eight Diagram Palm," it does not focus on the palm alone. In fact, every part of the body: fist, palm, elbow, shoulder, head, hip, knee and foot are trained to move and strike freely and continuously. Ba Gua is said to be characterized by "ambushing hands and hidden kicks." Within the forms and movements are Sixty-Four Hands, Seventy-Two Secret Kicks, as well as *Na Fa* (seizing methods), and *Shuai Fa* (throwing methods).

Ba Gua & Military Strategy

Ba Gua Zhang has been likened to guerilla warfare because its chosen tactic is to evade and counterattack, or to escape and let the opponent fall into emptiness. Ba Gua specializes in using footwork to move out of the line of the

---

[3] *The Propensity of Things: Toward a History of Efficacy in China,* Francois Jullien (New York: Zone Books, 1999) p. 151.

attack and then counterattacking against the opponent's weak point, rather than confronting him directly. To illustrate this idea, many Ba Gua practitioners are fond of quoting ancient classics on military strategy and Ma Ze Dong's famous sixteen-character poem explaining his tactics of guerilla warfare:

When the enemy advances, we retreat!

When the enemy halts, we harass!

When the enemy seeks to avoid battle, we attack!

When the enemy retreats, we pursue!

These ideas are also present in many of the oral instructions that are considered critical to understanding and correct training in Ba Gua.

Ba Gua Zhang as a Physical Discipline & Spiritual Path

Although Ba Gua Zhang is a martial art, for many practitioners its most important facet is its ability to promote health and deeper engagement with the world. In this sense Ba Gua Zhang provides a template for integrating body, mind and spirit. The foundation of spiritual health is physical and mental health. Ba Gua Zhang's emphasis on creating internal harmony and balance, self-cultivation of mind and body, and adapting to change can help one to more easily negotiate life and interactions with others. Ba Gua's martial tactic of changing with the changing circumstances, or as some people say: "going with the flow," helps us to understand and adapt to the natural world, and its manifestations within us. The seasons, weather, the harmony and majesty of nature with its unending cycles of growth flourishing, decay and renewal are constantly changing and these changes affect us and move through us. Understanding change also helps us understand how to have a healthy relationship with ourselves and with others, so that we can adapt to different situations and cultures.

Ba Gua Zhang provides practitioners with an embodied spirituality and philosophy based on ancient principles that have withstood the test of time, and can help us to be in tune with ourselves and the world around us. Regular practice of Ba Gua Zhang develops a singular mindfulness that improves one's health and approach to living. From a Daoist perspective, Ba Gua reconnects us to the "Original Mind," an inner knowing or inner wisdom that is outside of analytical thinking mechanisms.

Master Gao Ji Wu in the Heaven Upholding Palm

Styles of Ba Gua Zhang

When Dong HaiChuan began to teach Ba Gua during the Qing dynasty, many accomplished martial arts practitioners studied with him, including Cheng Ting Hua, Song Yong Xiang, Liu De Kuan, Liang Chen Pu, Yin Fu, Ma Wei Qi, and Fan Zhi Yong. It is thought that Dong taught each student somewhat differently according to their natural physical attributes and previous martial arts training, and that later each disciple modified the principles they learned to suit their individual temperaments and abilities. For example, Cheng Ting Hua was already quite accomplished at wrestling and throwing techniques before studying with Dong. Hence, the "Dragon-Claw" palm is the basic palm shape of Cheng Style Ba Gua, perhaps because the rounded, stretched shape of the hand makes it more useful for grabbing and pulling opponents off balance in order to throw them. Yin Fu was a thinner man and had studied Lohan Shaolin. Yin Style Ba Gua emphasizes sidestepping and using a piercing palm to attack the opponent's vulnerable points. Liang Chen Pu studied not only with Dong but also with Cheng and Yin, so Liang Style Ba Gua combines elements of the both Yin Style and Cheng Style.

The Styles of Ba Gua Zhang that exist today are listed below. They are generally named after their founders. They all share the same underlying principles:

- Yin Style: Yin Fu (尹福)

- Cheng Style: Cheng Ting Hua (程廷華)

- Liang Style: Liang Zhen Pu (梁振蒲)

- Gao Style: Gao Yi Sheng (高義盛)

- Beijing Gao Style Ba Gua: Gao Wen Chang and Gao Zi Ying (高文成 and 高子英)

- Jiang Style: Jiang Rong Qiao (姜容樵)

- Shi Style: Shi Ji Dong (史计栋)

- Song Style: Song Chan Rong 宋长荣 & Song Yong Xiang (宋永祥)

- Fan Family Style: Fan Zhi Yong (范志勇)

- Liu Style: Liu Bao Zhen (劉寶珍)

- Ma Style: Ma Wei Qi (馬維棋)

- Ma Gui Style: Ma Gui (马贵)

- Gong Bao Tian Style: Gong Bao Tan (宮寶田)

- Sun Style: Sun Lu Tang (孫祿堂)

- Fu Style: Fu Zhen Song (傅振嵩)

- Yin Yang Style (or Tian Style): Tian Hui (田廻)

Teachers often study more than one style of Ba Gua during their lifetime. For example, although I have primarily studied with teachers in the Liang Zhen Pu Lineage I have also studied: Beijing Gao Style Ba Gua Zhang (A mix of Liang Style and Yin Style with other elements added), Gao Yi Sheng Style Ba Gua Zhang, Jiang Style Ba Gua Zhang, and Wu Jun Shan's Ba Gua (from Fu Shu Yun). I also studied Bai Yun (White Cloud) Ba Gua with Wes Tasker, who learned this art from Willem de Thouars

BA GUA & THE *YI JING* (BOOK OF CHANGES)

The *Yi Jing* has been part of Chinese culture and philosophy for more than four millennia. Its origins are connected with the mythological genesis of the Chinese people. The *Yi Jing* literally means the "Classic of Change." In the West the *Yi Jing* is often referred to as the "Book of Changes." The *Yi Jing* is based on the concept of Yin and Yang, which is a philosophy of both unity and opposition:

Heaven is Yang;	Earth is Yin
The Sun is Yang	The Moon is Yin
Light is Yang	Darkness is Yin
Male is Yang;	Female is Yin
Insubstantial is Yang	Substantial is Yin
Motion is Yang	Tranquility is Yin
Firmness is Yang	Gentleness is Yin
Above is Yang	Below is Yin
Hot is Yang	Cold is Yin

In the *Yi Jing,* Yin and Yang are used to express the idea of constant change and transformation. They are ideal concepts for this purpose because Yin and Yang themselves are not separate static states, but a dynamic unity, each dependent upon the other, always in flux, inter-transforming, inter-consuming, and infinitely divisible. The *Yi Jing* employs symbols, Yang represented by a solid line, and Yin by a broken line, in order to study inherent patterns or dispositions for change. By ordering Yin and Yang lines into groups of three, Eight Diagrams (*Ba Gua*) or Trigrams are produced. These Trigrams, and expanded six-line diagrams called Hexagrams, are used to interpret natural phenomena, human archetypes, the growth and decline of systems, the changing potentialities of success in a given situation, or the patterns of change inherent in virtually any phenomena. Modern authors have commented on the similarity between *Yi Jing* symbols and binary code. The Eight Trigrams are traditionally organized into two patterns. The first arrangement purportedly created by Fu Xi at the dawn of Chinese civilization is called the Pre-Heaven Arrangement:

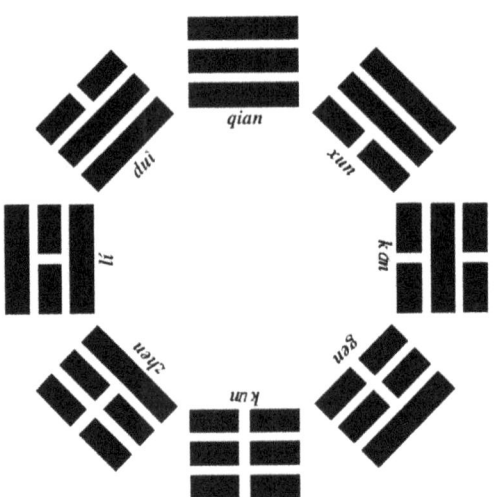

This arrangement presents the fundamental energetic forces in the universe as oppositional polarities. Over a thousand years later King Wen is credited with creating another arrangement, which reflects the cyclical changes that characterize terrestrial life: day and night, the changing seasons, birth and death. This is called the Post-Heaven Arrangement:

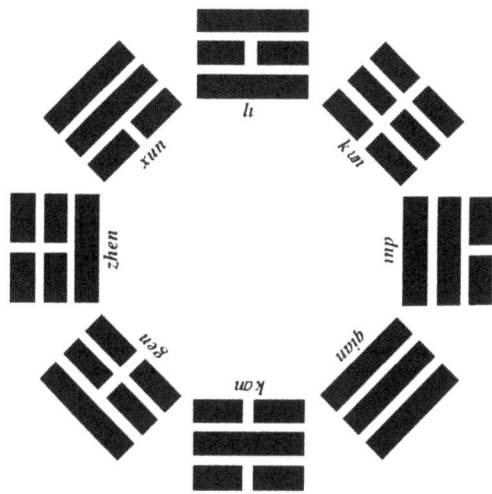

Each force or principle is given a symbolic name, which has various connotations:

Qian Diagram

Name: The Creative

Image: Heaven

Nature: Creativity; Strength; Vigor

Trigram: Qian is 3 links (*Qian San Lian*).

Kun Diagram

Name: The Receptive

Image: Earth

Nature: Yielding; Receptivity

Trigram: Kun is Separated into Six Sections (*Kun Liu Duan*)

Zhen Diagram

Name: The Arousing

Image: Thunder

Nature: Exciting; Arousing; Inciting Movement

Trigram: Zhen is an Upturned Jar (*Zhen Yang Yu*)

Gen Diagram

Name: Keeping Still

Image: Mountain

Nature: Immovable; Stubborn

Trigram: Gen is a Toppled Bowl (*Gen Fu Wan*)

Li Diagram

Name: The Clinging

Image: Fire

Nature: Attachment

Trigram: Li is Empty in the Middle (*Li Zhong Xu*)

Kan Diagram

Name: The Abysmal

Image: Water

Nature: Enveloping; Dangerous

Trigram: Kan is Full in the Middle (*Kan Zhong Man*)

Dui Diagram

Name: The Joyous

Image: Lake

Nature: Joy; Pleasure

Trigram: Dui Lacks in the Top (*Dui Shang Que*)

Xun Diagram

Name: The Gentle

Image: Wind

Nature: Penetrating; Enduring

Trigram: Xun is Broken in the Bottom (*Xun Xia Duan*)

Over time *Yi Jing* concepts were applied not only to understanding natural phenomena, but also to such varied fields as divination, Chinese medicine, military strategy, the martial arts and Daoist longevity exercises. Because the *Yi Jing* was influential in so many facets of Chinese culture, it is fairly certain that the founder of Ba Gua Zhang, Dong Hai

Chuan, was influenced by these ideas in creating and structuring this new martial art. The Post-Heaven arrangement of the Trigrams is of particular importance to Ba Gua practitioners, because of its focus on terrestrial forces, cyclical change and the eight directions. The influence of the *Yi Jing* on Ba Gua Zhang is evident in the following areas:

1. Military Strategy

By the time Dong formulated his art in the late Qing dynasty, the Trigrams and Hexagrams of the *Yi Jing* had been used for centuries by military officers and martial artists to symbolize certain principles of military strategy. For example, "make noise in the East to attack the West," a basic principle of guerilla warfare, which today forms one of the strategies of Ba Gua Zhang, was associated with the Cui Hexagram (Gathering Together). "The Cicada Sheds its Skin," describes the strategy of feigning inaction, while taking action in secret. It is associated with the Gu Hexagram (Arresting Decay). This idea is reflected in the movement "Golden Cicada Sheds Skin" one of the 64 palms, the linear Ba Gua Zhang fighting applications.

2. Chinese Medicine

Yi Jing principles were applied to the practice and theory of Chinese medicine as early as the Han Dynasty (202 BC to AD 220). The Trigrams and their arrangements became associated with various parts of the body and the internal organs. The circulation of *Qi* (the vital energy), blood and fluids also came to be explained in terms of the Trigrams and the relationship to the internal organs and the Five Elements (*Wu Xing*). Correspondences were made between the meridians and points used in acupuncture and the Eight Trigrams, leading to the creation of *Yi Jing* based acupuncture methods.

3. Daoist Health Practices

Manuscripts from the early Han dynasty unearthed at the Mawangdui tomb site in Hunan Province demonstrate that formalized practice of *Dao Yin* internal exercises and *Tu Na* (breathing exercises) began more than 2,000 years ago. These early practices were refined over the centuries, and became part of Daoist and Buddhist spiritual practices as well as martial arts training regimens. The key element in many of these practices is a transformation of the body's vital energies, sometimes referred to as "internal alchemy." In particular this involves replenishing the *Jing* (essence) and transforming *Jing* into *Qi* and *Qi* into *Shen* (Spirit). This transformative process, symbolized by the Li (Fire) and Kan (Water) Trigrams, is achieved through quieting the mind, and guiding the *Qi* with the breath and the intention. Some of these practices are integrated into Ba Gua Zhang.

4. Tactics & Body Alignment In Combat

Ba Gua Zhang as a fighting art is based upon understanding the nature of Yin and Yang as oppositional forces that form a dynamic unity undergoing continuous change and transformation. These principles are manifest in the Ba Gua's emphasis on:

1. **Simultaneously Experiencing Motion & Tranquility**: When the body is in motion, there is stillness and tranquility within. When the body is still, there is hidden movement within.

2. **Simultaneous Manifestation of Firmness & Gentleness:** Firm power and gentle, yielding force mutually coexist. This combination of the firm and yielding allows one to adapt to changing situations and adjust accordingly.

3. **Employing Endless Changes in Order to Adapt to the Moment:** "From one *Qi* turning, a thousand things appear, from one technique, a thousand can be created."

4. **Footwork:** In Ba Gua Zhang emphasis is placed on footwork, and being able to freely move and turn to face the eight directions. These directions are represented by the Eight Trigrams. The use of circular footwork allows one to observe all eight directions with a single step. At the same time, the footwork in conjunction with the movements of the hands and waist allow one to respond and generate power to the eight directions: high and low, front and back, right and left, turning inward and turning outward.

The Eight Trigrams are Often Used as Symbols to Describe Internal Body Alignments: The broken and solid lines represent areas of the body that are relatively empty or full of *Qi* and Intention. For Example:

Qian Diagram: Qian is 3 links (*Qian San Lian*): The eyes should not leave the hand, the hand should not leave the elbow and the elbow should not leave the ribs. These are the three links in the Qian diagram.

Kun Diagram: Kun is Six Sections (*Kun Liu Duan*): In walking, the movements of the lower limbs employ the hips knees and feet. These six sections of the body relate to the six sections in Kun diagram.

Zhen Diagram: An Upturned Bowl (*Zhen Yang Yu*): Tightening strength in the two shoulders, lifting the perineum and rounding the hip are represented by a supine broad-mouthed bowl, the Zhen diagram.

Gen Diagram: Gen is a Toppled Bowl (*Gen Fu Wan***):** Uplifting the neck and touching the upper palate with the tongue are represented by the solid upper line in the Gen diagram.

Li Diagram: Li is Empty in the Middle (*Li Zhong Xu***):** The upper back is erect and the chest is gently hollowed and relatively empty in relation to the lower abdomen. This relaxes the diaphragm and calms the Heart. These alignments are represented by the broken, middle line in the Li diagram.

Kan Diagram: Kan is Full in the Middle (*Kan Zhong Man***):** Sinking *Qi* into the *Dantian* area below the navel. This strengthens the body. Being relatively full in the lower abdomen is represented by the solid, middle line in the Kan diagram.

Dui Diagram: Dui Lacks in the Top (*Dui Shang Que***):** The configuration of the Dui diagram, represents the basin-like structure of the pelvis, firmly supported by the hips and legs.

Xun Diagram: Xun is Broken in the Bottom (*Xun Xia Duan***):** The Xun trigram's broken lower line represents the mobility of the legs and the hooking (*Kou Bu*) and swinging (*Bai Bu*) steps of the feet, with the knees closed to protect the groin.

Yi Jing Philosophy and Ba Gua Zhang

The philosophy of the *Yi Jing* was adopted by practitioners of Ba Gua, and to some degree the practice of Ba Gua is an embodied manifestation of the approach to life and change espoused in the *Yi Jing*. One of the challenges every human being experiences is to move through life with all its unpredictable changes, its summits and depths, as smoothly and gracefully as possible. Change is part of who we are, and it is, to some degree, what makes us who we are. Change confronts us and our reaction to it shapes us. To adapt to change requires an ongoing process of self-cultivation and self-education. The *Yi Jing* has a very practical orientation in its approach to change. It teaches us about change and engages with the many facets of human life in order to help us understand, adapt to, and flow with uncertainty and change. Although the *Yi Jing* is a book of vast depth, and has been subjected to extensive commentary and interpretation, which sometimes confound as much as they elucidate, recurring themes and ideas permeate the text. These can be understood as general principles of living life in an ever-changing world.

Change can be sudden, but often it starts slowly and almost imperceptibly. If one can identify that the situation is shifting before events unfold completely, it is possible to adapt to events and even shape them when they are small and easier to handle. Once the changes are fully underway, it is more difficult to adjust to and shape events. Adaptation requires awareness, flexibility and self-cultivation. The practice of Ba Gua Zhang can help us to develop these qualities, laying the groundwork and preparing us for the adaptations we must make.

Practicing Ba Gua Zhang sensitizes the individual to the process of change and transformation. As a martial art, Ba

Gua Zhang embodies the idea of having a guiding intention, but no fixed plans, except to change appropriately with the changing circumstances (dictated by the terrain, energy and specific configuration of a particular encounter), in order to prevail. This ability can only manifest itself when there is internal harmony and alignment. In Ba Gua Zhang internal harmony is attributed to unity of the Heart-Mind and Intention (*Yi*) with *Qi* (vital force), and *Qi* with *Jin*. Heart-Mind and *Qi* can be understood as one's internal configuration or disposition. *Jin* is an extension of the internal configuration, which can be expressed as force and power, energy and spirit. *Jin* transforms constantly, manifesting differently from moment to moment, changing according to the situation. These interactions and transformations occur largely on an implicit level, while the physical body responds in coordination with internal unity and harmony. In Ba Gua Zhang, each moment of the encounter dictates the next as the opponent's *Jin* interacts with your own.

As a mind-body discipline, Ba Gua Zhang trains one to experience and sense the continuous changes and transformations that flow from the internal unity of Heart-Mind, *Yi*, *Qi* and *Jin*. The postures and movements of Ba Gua Zhang simultaneously arouse and enliven the *Qi*, so that there is no gap between intention and action, and open the body's energy pathways so that they are unblocked and free-flowing. This creates the basis for developing a sensitized awareness of transformation and change. Flowing with the moment-to-moment changes in the body allows one to experience and sense the most minute changes in the internal configuration - an ability to sense the first stirrings of a transformation. The changes in our internal body pattern and the configuration of the *Qi* internally also interact with what is external - the *Qi* of the surrounding environment, which includes the *Qi* configurations of the people and things we are interacting with.

Ba Gua Zhang employs arcing circular steps. Its basic practice is to walk in circles. In circling, one is continuously changing and turning, simultaneously advancing and retreating with every step, always circling back to the beginning. This is not starting over, but rather a series of renewals. Like the turning of the seasons, each return and each renewal is unique, each return brings something new. The necessary disposition for change and transformation is generated internally and expressed externally, constantly renewed and strengthened through endless cycles that never repeat, but continuously loop. What is generated internally is manifested externally. This constant renewal and fine-tuned sensitivity to the subtle changes in the interplay between your own internal configuration, and that of the people and events around you, creates space and opportunity for positive transformation.

BA GUA ZHANG & DAOISM

Chinese martial arts are all, to some degree, influenced by the "Three Schools" - Daoism, Confucianism and Buddhism. Internal arts like Ba Gua Zhang, Tai Ji Quan and Xing Yi Quan are no exception, however these arts also draw very heavily on Daoist philosophy, language and imagery, as well as Daoist self-cultivation, health, and longevity practices that have been imbedded in Chinese culture for at least two thousand years.

The primary internal exercise in Ba Gua Zhang is to walk in a circle holding fixed postures. This practice is known as *Ding Shi Ba Gua Zhang*. It is believed that Dong Hai Chuan, the founder of Ba Gua Zhang, synthesized the best of various martial styles in order to create Ba Gua. However the key element of this new style was the practice of walking in a circle while holding various postures that energize and strengthen the body while simultaneously calming the mind and refining and purifying the spirit. Historical evidence shows that that Dong probably studied with the Dragon Gate (*Long Men*) school, part of the Complete Reality (*Quan Zhen*) sect of Daoism, which practiced a form of Daoist circle walking meditation.

These Daoist practitioners practiced a method of circle walking meditation in order to open and harmonize the meridians of the body, promote health and focus and quiet the mind. They also used this practice, called "Rotating in the Worship of Heaven," not for martial purposes, but to refine *Qi* and Spirit through external movement in order to realize internal stillness or emptiness (ie: the Dao). There is a paragraph in the Daoist Canon that says:

A person's heart and mind are in chaos,

Concentration on one thing makes the mind pure.

If one aspires to reach the Dao,

One should practice walking in a circle.[4]

Daoist adepts from the *Long Men* School walked the circle with smooth natural steps without bobbing or leaning. As they walked they chanted mantras like: *When rotating in the worship of Heaven, the sound of thunder is everywhere and transforms everything.*[5] Some modern practitioners of Circle Walking Meditation silently chant words like, "Relax," "Calm Myself," "Emptiness," or "Silent in Myself." Sometimes the chant is coordinated with the breath, so that one inhales on one word and exhales on the next word. For example, saying: "Relax" on the inhale, and "Myself" on the exhale. Purportedly Dong saw that circle walking had value, not only as a meditation and health exercise, but also as the foundation of an effective method of martial arts that allowed the practitioner to deliver powerful strikes while in constant motion.

Some of Ba Gua's meditation, breathing and Nei Gong practices are derived from both Daoist and Buddhist methods of self cultivation, because they cultivate a state of relaxed awareness, strengthen the body and promote health, all necessary pre-requisites for martial arts training. Many of these practices are rooted in Daoist imagery and cosmology. The Ba Gua Diagram represents the balance of the different forces or energies in the universe and serves as a metaphor for finding balance and harmony within ourselves. The principles of understanding and adapting to change expressed in the *Yi Jing*, a text in the Daoist Canon, have a

---

[4] *The Origins of Pa Kua Chang Part 3*, by Dan Miller and Kang Ge Wu (Pa Kua Chang Journal Vol. 3, No. 4 May/June 1993) p. 27.
[5] Ibid, p.27-29.

particular resonance with practitioners of an art based on circular movements, and continuous movement and change.

Ba Gua Zhang, like Tai Ji Quan and Xing Yi Quan, has adopted Daoist philosophical ideas that have important implications for both the martial and psycho-spiritual aspects of the art. Three of these concepts that are particularly relevant to Ba Gua Zhang are discussed below.

Water as a Metaphor for the Dao

Water has a number of symbolic associations with the Dao. Water is the nourishing source of life. Water flows and is constantly changing from moment to moment. Its movement is natural and spontaneous. There is no force that moves water, it simply spreads in all directions adapting its form to the terrain. Like the Dao, water is shapeless and formless, yet it is powerful. Water cannot be grasped, it is yielding, yet it "overcomes the hard" because it penetrates through rock and can dissolve other substances.

It is easy to see why in Chinese military strategy, and in Ba Gua Zhang, one is advised to be like water. Water is flexible, adaptable, always changing and flowing. When one attempts to block water, it flows around the obstacle, never confronting it head on. Water does not move in straight lines but rushes, spirals and eddies unpredictably. It is substantial, yet when one attempts to grasp it, it slips away. Water is soft and yielding, yet it is powerful like a pounding wave, containing a heavy mass of water that can exert tremendous force. *The Art of War*, a military treatise based on Daoist principles says that:

> *Water shapes its current*
>
> *From the lie of the land.*
>
> *The warrior shapes his victory*

From the dynamic of the enemy.[6]

The skilled general or martial artist follows these principles. Like water, the general flows around obstacles, insinuating himself, or "leaking" into the smallest openings, always taking the line of least resistance.

The inner stillness associated with mediation and self-realization is often compared to the clarity of still water. When water is still, it reflects, acting as a mirror through which we can see the world and ourselves clearly. In Chinese thought, the primary image of the Heart-Mind is that of a pool of water, which is clear and reflective when it is still, but becomes cloudy when stirred up. Emotions stir up the Heart-Mind so that it becomes cloudy and confused. Stilling the mind, so that it is calm, returns clarity of thought and insight.

The Analogy of the Wheel

The Dao De Jing, probably the most well known Daoist text compares the Dao to a wheel:

> *We put thirty spokes together and call it a wheel; but it is on the space where there is nothing that the usefulness of the wheel depends.*

The spokes of the wheel of a cart turn around the hub, which remains still in the center. It keeps its position by being still and "doing nothing," yet it is through doing nothing that the spokes can actively and harmoniously turn. Circular rotation requires a pivot, and without this unmoving pivot, the wheel will go out of balance.

Ba Gua teachers say that in walking the circle, externally there is movement and internally one is still. Rotation is the

---

[6]*The Art of War*, by Sun Tzu, translated by John Minford. (New York: Penguin Books, 2009).

heart of Ba Gua. Some practitioners liken the whole body to the universe, in which every part is constantly rotating in relation to all the other parts, like wheels within wheels. The whole body relaxes and turns so that each part can store and release power by continuously winding and un-winding. The famous Ba Gua Practitioner Cheng Ting Hua said that the practitioner rotates his body like a small screw and hub. In Ba Gua Zhang, the center of the lower back (*Yao*) is like the hub, the axis of the movements. The hands and feet and the rest of the body are like spokes and the curved surface of the wheel. When the body moves, the *Yao* and more specifically the internal area behind the center of the lower back, the *Mingmen* must move first. It drives and leads everything. Therefore the *Mingmen* is the inner point of stillness around which the rest of the body moves, just as the Dao is eternal and unchanging. As the body moves and changes, the mind and spirit stay relaxed, calm and still.

Wu Wei (Non-Doing) & *Zi Ran* (Spontaneity)

The Daoist idea of non-action, non-interference and non-intervention is called *Wu Wei*. *Wu Wei* does not actually mean doing nothing at all. It does not signify the complete absence of activity, but rather not overdoing - doing less, and acting without artificiality or arbitrariness. This also means not interfering with the patterns and rhythms of nature, not imposing our own intentions on the organization of the world. Our senses, desires and actions can lead us astray. In trying to satisfy them, we lose sight of the relative importance of things, and of our own inner nature and individual capacity.

Not-doing can also be understood as spontaneity (*Zi Ran*). *Zi Ran* is sometimes translated as nature, natural or spontaneity. It literally means "self-so" Through decreasing and doing less, one returns to one's inner nature. In both Daoist and Confucian thought, water is often used as an example of the inherent power contained in *Wu Wei*. As we saw above, water does not "take action" in an of itself, but moves in accordance with the terrain and circumstances, naturally, powerfully and inexorably, flowing downward, transforming itself from spring, to stream, to tributary, to river and to sea, carrying with it a endless life giving force.

Deliberate movement of the Heart-Mind is related to the Intention (*Yi*). When the intention and Qi, move naturally and spontaneously, like water following its natural course, then, Intention and *Qi* are in harmony with one's nature and therefore in harmony with the Dao. Because breathing is linked to *Qi*, breathing naturally, deeply, and completely links one to the Original Mind and Original Spirit, particularly as the breath becomes refined and soft. The movement of *Qi* is often likened to the movement of water. Just as water evaporates, gathers in the clouds and falls back to earth to accumulate in lakes and rivers, so too do *Qi* and breath rise and fall in the body like a fine mist ceaselessly coalescing and dispersing. Both water and the Heart-Mind undergo a similar series of transformations, and both are clarified and replenished through these ceaseless, cyclical processes.

These ideas relating to spontaneous natural movement and effortless action are part of Ba Gua Zhang and the other internal martial arts. By blending with the opponent's movements, one moves naturally and effortlessly without struggling or exerting excessive effort. One's daily practice also manifests these qualities. Cultivation of *Qi*, breath and internal alignment cannot be forced, Rather than over-training or trying to force progress, one lets things develop in their own time, while attending to, and watching, one's internal processes. Part of what we are trying to learn in the internal martial arts is how to reconnect to our own spontaneous and instinctive movement as it manifests both internally or externally. This involves a careful balancing of rigorous, focused practice, and a non-interfering observing and "letting go."

HEALTH BENEFITS OF BA GUA ZHANG

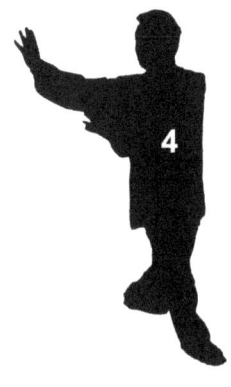

The primary internal exercise in Ba Gua Zhang (Eight Diagram Palm) is to walk in a circle holding fixed postures. This practice is known as *Ding Shi Ba Gua Zhang* (Fixed Pattern Eight Diagram Palm. Dong Hai Chuan, the founder of Ba Gua Zhang, synthesized the best of various martial styles in order to create Ba Gua. However the key element of this new style was the practice of walking in a circle holding various postures that energize and strengthen the body, while calming the mind and refining and purifying the spirit.

The effects of circular walking have been noticed by modern researchers who observed that walking a circle seemed to create relaxation and stress reduction through its concentration and focus on the center of the circle. Some researchers think that circle walking may also balance the two sides of the brain, because circle walking, with its directional shifts from clockwise to counterclockwise seems to increase activity in the corpus collosum, which connects the two hemispheres of the brain.

Dong saw that this circle walking Practice had value not only as a meditation and health exercise, but also as the foundation of an effective method of martial arts As a result the following statement is attributed to Dong Hai Chuan:

Training in martial arts ceaselessly is inferior to walking the circle. In Ba Gua Zhang circle walking practice is the font of all training.

Walking as Exercise

Modern research has only recently confirmed something that the Chinese clearly knew over a thousand years ago – that regular moderate exercise enhances resistance to disease, improves emotional well being and reduces the incidence and risk of high blood pressure, strokes and diseases like diabetes. Studies have shown that a moderate exercise like walking may actually produce greater results than more intensive cardio-vascular exercise. As proof, some doctors point to the work of Hiroshi Nose:

Hiroshi Nose, M.D., Ph.D., a professor of sports medical sciences at Shinshu University Graduate School of Medicine in Japan, who has enrolled thousands of older Japanese citizens in an innovative, five-month-long program of brisk, interval-style walking (three minutes of fast walking, followed by three minutes of slower walking, repeated 10 times). The results have been striking. "Physical fitness - maximal aerobic power and thigh muscle strength - increased by about 20 percent," Dr. Nose wrote in an e-mail, "which is sure to make you feel about 10 years younger than before training." The walkers' "symptoms of lifestyle-related diseases (hypertension, hyperglycemia and obesity) decreased by about 20 percent," he added, while their depression scores dropped by half. Walking has also been shown by other researchers to aid materially in weight control. A 15-year study found that middle-aged women who walked for at least an hour a day maintained their weight over the decades. Those who didn't gained weight. In addition, a recent seminal study found that when older people started a regular program of brisk walking, the volume of their hippocampus, a portion of the brain involved in memory, increased significantly.[7]

Walking is superior to many other forms of exercise, because it balances the musculature of the legs and utilizes the entire body through the natural oppositional movements of the arms and legs and their concomitant production of spiral movements through the torso, which in turn relaxes the diaphragm and engages the inter-costal and stomach muscles. This in turn stimulates the organs of digestion and improves circulation throughout the entire body.

Qi Gong and Nei Gong: The Benefit of Internal Exercise

Internal Exercises like Qi Gong and Nei Gong and martial arts like Ba Gua Zhang and Tai Ji Quan, which feature slow deliberate movements performed in conjunction with deep breathing and focused mind-intention have been shown to produce a multitude of improvements in physiological functioning and resistance to disease:

---

[7] *What's the Single Best Exercise?* by Gretchen Reynolds (Published: April 15, 2011 New York Times Magazine)
http://www.nytimes.com/2011/04/17/magazine/mag-17exercise-t.html

- One study showed that Qi Gong exercise has been shown to increase blood flow to the brain, creating improvements in symptoms such as memory, dizziness, and insomnia.[8]

- A study of people with high blood pressure showed that after 12 weeks of Qi Gong, blood pressure and cholesterol levels were lower.

- A study in Korea indicated that regular practice of Qi Gong reduced blood pressure, as well as reduced cortisol levels. Cortisol is produced by the adrenal gland and is often referred to as the "stress hormone" as it is involved in response to stress.[9]

- In the treatment of asthma, self-applied Qi Gong led to significant cost decreases, such as reduction in sick days, hospitalization days, emergency consultations, respiratory tract infections, and the number of drugs and drug costs.[10]

- Unfavorable changes of sex hormone levels due to aging were retarded by regular practice of Qi Gong exercises.

- Superoxide dismutase (SOD), an anti-aging enzyme that is produced naturally by the body, declines with age. SOD is believed to destroy free radicals that may

---

[8] *What's the Single Best Exercise?* by Gretchen Reynolds (Published: April 15, 2011 New York Times Magazine)
http://www.nytimes.com/2011/04/17/magazine/mag-17exercise-t.html
[9] *Qigong Reduced Blood Pressure and Catecholamine Levels of Patients with Essential Hypertension,* by Myung-Suk Lee, Myeong Soo Lee et als (2003, Vol. 113, No. 12) p. 1691-1701.
http://informahealthcare.com/doi/abs/10.1080/00207450390245306
[10] Multifaceted Health Benefits of Medical Qigong, by Kenneth M. Sancier, Ph.D. and Devatara Holman MS, MA (Lac J. Alt Compl Med. 2004; 10(1)) p.163-166.

cause aging. In one study the SOD levels of retired workers who did Qi Gong exercises showed that the mean level of SOD was increased by Qi Gong exercise.[11]

- A study sponsored by the National Institute on Aging and National Center for Complementary and Alternative Medicine compared the effects of Qi Gong and Tai Ji, on adults 60 and older, measuring their immunity to the Varicella Zoster Virus that causes shingles. After 12 weeks, the participants had raised their immunity to the virus.

- Regular practice of Qi Gong can improve sleep and reduce daytime fatigue and drowsiness.

- Qi Gong and Tai Ji Quan have been shown to reduce stress and psychological distress.

- The practice of Qi Gong has been shown to reduce arthritis pain and stiffness in the joints. Regular practice of Qi Gong helped patients reduce their pain medication.[12]

- A clinical trial at Tufts Medical Center found that after 12 weeks of Tai Ji Quan, patients with Fibromyalgia, a chronic pain condition, did significantly better in measurements of pain, fatigue, physical functioning, sleeplessness and depression than a comparable group given stretching exercises and wellness education. Tai Ji Quan patients were

---

[11] Anti-Aging Benefits of Qigong, by Kenneth Sancier Ph. D., http://www.qigonginstitute.org/html/papers/Anti-Aging_Benefits_of_Qigong.html
[12] *Effects of Qigong Therapy on Arthritis: A Review and Report of a Pilot Trial* by Kevin W Chen and Tianjun Liu. (Medical Paradigm: June 2004 – Volume 1, Number 1); www.wishus.org/researchpapers/Arthritis.pdf

also more likely to sustain improvement three months later.[13]

Meditation and Breathing

Qi Gong exercises and Ba Gua Zhang employ various methods of regulating the breath to enhance power, harmonize the flow of *Qi* and calm and quiet the mind, so that distracting thoughts are put aside for the duration of the practice session. This phenomenon has been labeled "the relaxation response" by researchers like Herbert Benson. Benson found that this mind-body state, common to various methods of meditation and exercises like Qi Gong and Ba Gua Zhang, could counteract the harmful effects of stress and the flight or fight response. Benson also found that many of the following conditions could be significantly improved or cured when people regularly engage in a practice that produces the "relaxation response":[14]

- Constipation
- Cardiac Arrhythmia
- Herpes Simplex
- Bronchial Asthma
- Diabetes
- Duodenal ulcers
- Hypertension
- Insomnia
- Pain

---

[13] *Tai Chi Reported to Ease Fibromyalgia,* by Pam Belluck (The New York Times, August 18, 2010).
http://www.nytimes.com/2010/08/19/health/19taichi.html

[14] *The Relaxation Response,* By Herbert Benson MD, (New York: HarperCollins, 2000. First Published in 1975 by William Morrow and Co. Inc).
p. xli-xlii.

More recently, researchers report that those who meditated for about thirty minutes a day for eight weeks had measurable changes in gray-matter density in parts of the brain associated with memory, sense of self, empathy and stress. M.R.I. brain scans taken before and after the participants' meditation regimen found increased gray matter in the hippocampus, an area important for learning and memory. The images also showed a reduction of gray matter in the amygdala, a region connected to anxiety and stress.[15]

Ba Gua Zhang & Respiration

The slow rhythmic deep abdominal breathing common to Ba Gua Zhang and Qi Gong and Nei Gong exercises is also an important element in their efficacy in promoting health and resistance to disease. Breathing "is" life. While we can go without food and water for days, we cannot go without breathing for even a few minutes. This most basic life rhythm has profound effects on the whole human organism. The movements of the diaphragm and ribs in inhalation and exhalation help the vena cava to return blood to the heart. Additionally, as the organs of digestion have direct and indirect attachments to the diaphragm, its piston-like action in breathing aids digestion and peristalsis. Even the kidneys move slightly with every breath. It is no surprise that impaired breathing can have profound affects on the functioning of the internal organs. It has been clinically shown that slow, even breathing at a rate of less than ten breaths per minute can modulate blood pressure. Regular practice of slowed breathing actually produced a drop in blood pressure of 20-30 points. The FDA has approved biofeedback-like devices that aid patients in slowing their

---

[15] *How Meditation May Change the Brain*, by Sindya N. Bhanoo (January 28, 2011, New York Times) http://well.blogs.nytimes.com/2011/01/28/how-meditation-may-change-the-brain/

breathing in order to treat hypertension. Recent studies indicate that slow, deliberate, relaxed breathing ("paced respiration") alone can make significantly reduce hot flashes in menopausal women.[16] Other confirmed benefits of slow, relaxed, deep breathing include reduced incidence of asthma and bronchitis, as well as increased lung capacity and stamina.

Many students who practice Nei Gong and Ba Gua Zhang experience large improvements in lung capacity and oxygen uptake. One very fit student who walks and bikes frequently found that biking up hills left him out of breath. His lung capacity, while good, was a little below the average. After several months of Ba Gua Zhang training his lung capacity was off the charts, and he no longer had trouble biking up hills. Another student reported that her oxygen consumption when scuba diving improved immensely. Her dive companions now ran out of oxygen long before she did.

Circle Walking Nei Gong

Ding Shi Ba Gua Zhang (the Nei Gong practice associated with the martial art Ba Gua Zhang) is unique as it combines the benefits of walking with the internal movements, correct body alignment, the deep abdominal breathing associated with Nei Gong and Qi Gong practices, as well as the relaxed and calm Mind-Intention of meditation and the relaxation response. Practitioners like Zhao Da Yuan and his teacher Li Zi Ming feel that Ba Gua in general, and Circle Walking in particular, are the ultimate Nei Gong exercise because they are the culmination of a tradition of *Dao Yin* (guiding, pulling and leading *Qi* exercises), *Tu Na* (breathing exercises), Nei Gong (internal exercises), martial arts, Daoist meditation and Daoist alchemical practices, and other *Yang*

---

[16] "Paced Respiration for Hot Flashes?" by Debra S. Burns, PhD, MT-BC; Janet S. Carpenter, PhD, RN, FAAN. (*The Female Patient* | VOL 37 JULY/AUGUST 2012). Online at. www.femalepatient.com

Sheng (Life Nourishing) practices that have their roots in methods developed in the early Han Dynasty (200 BCE). Because of the late development of Ba Gua Zhang as a martial art (the founder, Dong Hai Chuan, lived from 1813 to 1882), it draws on all of these traditions, and according to some experts, incorporated the best methods from these various traditions into its techniques and training methods.

Universal Movement

Both Zhao Da Yuan and Li Zi Ming feel that Ba Gua's Circle Walking Nei Gong practice conforms more completely with the intrinsic movement of the universe and the natural world than other forms of exercise. To paraphrase Li Zi Ming:

> *The movements of the celestial bodies in the universe contain both rotation and circulation. The human body is a microcosm of the universe – a small heavenly circle. The theory of Ba Gua draws upon this observation of the heavenly bodies by using rotation and circulation through its walking and turning practice. This practice harmonizes the practitioner with the natural movement of Qi of the universe. Ba Gua's practice of walking and rotating therefore conforms to the natural principle of the world around us. By walking the circle and rotating the body, Qi is aroused and circulates inside the body. This in turn strengthens the body, improves circulation and resistance to disease, and improves the functioning of the respiratory and digestive systems. Additionally, it produces a unified strength that stems from the arousal of the Qi. This strength can then be employed in the martial arts.[17]*

Walking the circle as a Ba Gua Nei Gong practice is not simply walking. It combines the benefits of walking with Qi

---

[17] *A Brief Introduction to the Body Strengthening Function of the Eight Diagram Palm Qi Gong* by Li Zi Ming, Translated by Huang Guo Qi, (Pa Kua Chang Journal Vol. 5 No. 1 Nov./Dec. 1994, Pacific Grove CA: High View Publications) p. 17-19.

Gong, meditation, and body strengthening practices such as the Muscle-Tendon Change (*Yi Jin Jing*), in which muscle, sinews and joints a systematically twisted and relaxed in much the same way that an animal naturally "exercises" its body. Circle Walking Nei Gong also develops a refined strength that can be employed in martial arts and other physical activities. As the body turns, and rotates, the muscles, fascia and energy pathways of the body (the meridians) are stimulated by spiraling actions that engage the whole body. The deep abdominal breathing combines with the body alignments to connect the lower body to the waist and upper limbs so that the whole body can be sensed. Inside, the mind is quiet and observant and outside there is movement and rotation. This creates a refined strength that is combined with internal relaxation - akin to the natural and relaxed strength of a cat. Perhaps this is why Ba Gua practitioners place such a premium on walking. Li Zi Ming summarized the importance of walking and in particular Ba Gua Circle Walking Nei Gong by simply saying:

Hundreds of exercises are not as good as simply walking;
Walking is the master of hundreds of exercises. [18]

How Ba Gua Improves Health and Fitness & Promotes Longevity

Ba Gua is characterized by continuous stepping that is balanced, slow and smooth. The body "roots" into the ground with each step, as it moves continuously forward. The Mud Wading Step (*Tang Ni Bu*) is the basic training step and, when combined with breath, intention and proper body alignment, forms the basis of Ba Gua's Circle Walking Nei Gong practice. Imagining that you are walking in mud up to your knees, creates a "moving root," an internal sense of being "rooted" or "screwed into" the ground. At the same

---

[18] *Liang Zhen Pu Eight Diagram Palm* by Li Zi Ming; translated by Huang Guo Qi and compiled and edited by Vince Black. (Pacific Grove, CA: High View Publications, 1993) p. 21.

time, this method of walking balances the muscles on the inside, outside and front and back of the legs. This in turn helps to correct misalignments of the joints in the lower limb and makes one less prone to injury.

The slow Mud Walking Step fully engages the body in minutely controlling the weight shifts from one foot to the other, so that one is always in balance. Mud Stepping aligns the joints of the lower leg and forges a connection between the legs and the body's energy centers in *Dantian* and *Mingmen*. Because the body "sits down" as one walks, weight is loaded onto the legs. This strengthens the bones and joints.

Studies in China have shown that Ba Gua circle walking had effects that are different than normal walking. Twisting the body while lowering the center of gravity and walking develops strength in the legs and waist and improves circulation in the lower body. Ba Gua Zhang practice has been shown to improve muscle strength, endurance, response time, and overall agility. One Chinese study found that normal walking burns 300-360 calories an hour, while Ba Gua walking burns 600-1,000.[19] Another study compared old Ba Gua Masters in Beijing with healthy old people who had never practiced Ba Gua. The two groups performed the same exercise, twelve minutes of quick walking. Blood pressure, heart rate, skin temperature and other markers were measured. The Ba Gua group could walk more quickly, their heart rate was slower, and blood pressure was lower.[20]

---

[19] *The Internal Palms of Pa Kua Chang for Self Defense, Conditioning and Health,* by Adam Hsu. (Black Belt Magazine, May 1987, vol. 2, No. 5)
[20] *Liu Bin's Zhuang Gong Bagua Zhang,* by Zhang Jie with Richard Shapiro. (Berkeley: Blue Snake Books, 2008) p. 50.

Ba Gua Master Li Zi Ming felt that the circular, rotational movements, and clockwise and counter clockwise walking actions inherent in circle walking, both produce and arouse the internal *Qi*. Because *Qi* is the foundation of strength, and actually directs the body's expression of dynamic power, Circle Walking Nei Gong quickly strengthens the body by activating and arousing the Original (*Yuan*) *Qi* of the body. This in turn strengthens the constitution and expels pathogens, something that medicine alone cannot do.[21]

---

[21] *A Brief Introduction to the Body Strengthening function of Eight Diagram Palm Qi gong,* by Li Zi Ming, translated by Huang Guo Qi, (Pa Gua Chang Journal, vol. 5, no. 1 Nov/Dec 1995 High view Publications. Pacific Grove CA) p. 17-19.

Circulation

Combining stepping with holding postures that open and activate the meridians improves circulation of *Qi,* blood and fluids through the soft tissue and the energy channels (meridians). Because meridians are not merely "lines of energy," but include fascia and connective tissue, these tissues are stretched and strengthened. This creates a flexible, integral strength. Additionally neural connections are forged that link the arms and legs in spiral configurations that further increase the flow of fluid through the soft tissue. Tai Ji expert Mike Sigman feels that the earliest documented meridians, called the "Sinew Channels" or "Tendino-Muscular Meridians," are the pathways along which force is propagated through the body. These channels not only relate to modern anatomical notions about fascial connections that connect the body from top to bottom, but are in fact, a much more sophisticated model.

Flexibility & Strength

Ba Gua Zhang increases and maintains flexibility, not through stretching, but through aligned and relaxed movements. Soft tissue tension is a key factor that inhibits flexibility. Moving with proper alignment, and from the "inside-out," allows the body to slowly relax and learn which muscles actually need to be used in particular action and which can relax. This not only improves flexibility, but also creates functional efficient strength. A simple way to test this is to try and hit something hard or throw something hard. Then spend a few minutes moving your body through the hitting or throwing action in a very slow and relaxed fashion as you breathe slowly in the lower abdomen. Try hitting or throwing again while retaining a sense of this relaxation and you will be surprised at the increase in speed and power.

The fascial twisting that occurs in Ba Gua Zhang movements and exercises develops refined strength. This is much like twisting and weaving several cables or ropes together in order to create a stronger, unified entity. Spiral movements move in all directions at once, making them difficult to resist, as there is no single point of leverage. Additionally, spiral alignments and movements create a tensile strength that resists compression and distributes force equally throughout the body.

Part of Ba Gua Zhang Training involves traditional weaponry. Working with weapons improves one's body mechanics and also increases functional strength. It is like a form of mild weight training, however rather the isolating individual muscles or groups of muscles, the goal in working with weapons is to use the structure of the whole body to hold up and move the weapon. Each weapon has a different weight, shape, and mode of usage, so each weapon develops different facets of functional strength.

Coordination & Agility

Training in Ba Gua Zhang greatly enhances coordination and agility. The graceful, but powerful movements of the palm changes and animal forms develop agile steps and integrated coordination of the hands, legs and waist. Perhaps the most famous story of the founder Dong Hai Chuan involves serving tea. The Emperor gave a great feast and the palace grounds were crowded with many people so it was difficult for the servants to move about. However Dong was easily able to slip through the crowds leaping on and off the courtyard walls while balancing trays in each hand. Today Ba Gua students still practice "Serving Teacup" exercises, which loosen the shoulders and link the hand, waist and legs in spiral movements.

Many of the New York City students say that Ba Gua Zhang training helps them easily wend their way through crowded rush hour sidewalks, as one student put it, "like a fish swimming through water."

**Master Gao Ji Wu "Serving Teacups"
In the Double Palm Change**

Stress Relief

We think that modern life is stressful because of its remove from an imagined pastoral simplicity. While there is some truth to this, stress is not new. Even in Daoist texts written 2,000 years ago there are passages that seem to address the problem of chronic stress. This stress is not simply created by outside pressures (these have always existed), but by our reaction to them. Stress and the fight or flight response are ingrained reactions to new situation, job insecurity, money worries, multi-tasking, social responsibilities and/or threats (real or perceived), and resistance to change. Tight, tense muscles also help to create and perpetuate stress by imprinting stress activating body patterns into the neuromuscular system. These negative patterns are very hard to change without a body-centered practice.

In *The Relaxation Response*, Dr. Herbert Benson identifies stress as a very significant factor in a host of diseases and syndromes ranging from heart problems to headaches, anxiety, chronic pain, diabetes, and asthma. He advocates inward looking exercises like meditation. Practices of this kind elicit what he calls the "Relaxation Response." Benson list four factors that are important in achieving this state:

1. A quiet environment.

2. Attention and the elimination of distracting thoughts through a practice or mantra.

3. A passive non-judgmental attitude.

4. A comfortable, aligned body position.[22]

Ba Gua Instructor, Psychologist and Daoist practitioner Dr. Robert Santee says that in Daoism, chronic stress is viewed as being out of harmony with the inevitable and continual process of change and transformation. This blocks the movement and transformation of our breath and energy. The Daoist approach to dealing with stress is almost identical to Benson's, but adds breath cultivation and an inner observation and awareness that is ongoing. This is achieved through disciplines like Ba Gua Zang that blend body-centered practices with mindfulness. This combination empties the Heart-Mind and allows the individual to listen with his or her *Qi*, in order to engage with the world in a natural and balanced way.[23] One of the practices Dr. Santee

---

[22] *The Relaxation Response, b*y Herbert Benson MD (New York: HarperCollins, 2000. First Published in 1975 by William Morrow and Co. Inc).
[23] *The Tao of Stress: How to Calm, Balance and Simplify Your Life*, by Robert G. Santee. PhD (Oakland, CA: New Harbinger Publications Inc. 2013) p. 18-23.

recommends for decreasing stress and promoting inner harmony is mindful circle walking.

Master Zhao Da Yuan, who teaches Ba Gua and Qin Na in Beijing, says that people become stressed when they develop a conflict between their inner and outer worlds. He feels that methods of Nei Gong and meditation, like those found in Ba Gua Zhang, which allow one to "enter into stillness," can enable people to understand this kind of division and opposition, so that they can integrate the interior and exterior self.

> *The importance of "entering into stillness" is its role in regulating and rebalancing the body through breathing, relaxation, calming the Heart-Mind and harmonizing the Qi. Focusing intention and thought reduces the pressure impinging on the Heart-Mind. At the moment of entering into stillness, problems that are hidden become perceptible as feelings, or emotions: distress, pain, cold, heat, distending, numb, itchy, etc. By entering into stillness we can begin to regulate these experiences as they appear.*[24]

For Master Zhao, part of entering into stillness involves sensing internally – listening and looking inside the body in conjunction with relaxed, focused, deep breathing so that the movements of the *Qi* can be minutely perceived and naturally regulated.

---

[24] *Practical Qin Na Part 1: Explanation of the Qin Na Nine Heaven Secret Text,* by Zhao Da Yuan, translation by Huang Guo Qi and Tom Bisio. Edited by Tom Bisio. (Denver: Outskirts Press, 2015) p. 44-46.

Master Zhao Da Yuan

Imagination, Creativity and Sensitivity

Part of a healthy mental outlook is exercising imagination and creativity. In Chinese medicine this is intimately bound up with the health of the mind and organs. Practicing Ba Gua Zhang requires mental engagement with the movements and the internal connections and energies that the movements and postures facilitate and elicit. This engages the mind and strengthens the spirit. The process of visualizing and doing is part and parcel of learning Ba Gua Zhang and its various Nei Gong methods. Visualizing and doing strengthens one's ability to imagine and achieve.

Ba Gua Zhang like other internal energy practices, increases one's ability to sense minute internal changes. This allows one to sense when the body is out of balance, long before that imbalance manifests as illness or disease. This ability also helps in modulating one's responses to the environment, for example adjusting smoothly to loud noises or environmental challenges. How often have you felt irritated by hot weather, or upset that it is so cold out? Yet these external things have nothing to do with your internal state. I remember a story a veteran traveler to China told me. He was in a bus station, and an elderly Chinese man was sleeping calmly next to a loudspeaker blaring out bus announcements. When the man awoke, my acquaintance asked him how he could sleep with all the noise. The old man, bemused by the question, answered "but that had nothing to do with me."

Walking and Neuroplasticity

Neuroplasticity refers to the brain's ability to reorganize itself by forming new neural connections throughout one's life. Neuroplasticity allows the neurons (nerve cells) in the brain to compensate for injury and disease and to adjust their activities in response to new situations or to changes in their environment.

Walking has been shown to have incredible effects on the brain's Neuroplasticity. A study at the University of Iowa found that walking three times a week led to improvements in patients' Parkinsonian Movement symptoms, enhanced their mood, and decreased fatigue. *Walking was also a key contributor to a very simple program that reduced the risk of dementia by a staggering 60 percent. If any drug could do that it would be the most talked-about treatment in medicine.*[25] In Alzheimer's disease degenerative changes begin in the hippocampus, which starts to shrink, so that people lose short-term memory. Walking actually produced significant Hippocampal enlargement.[26]

There is every indication that the neuroplasticity of the brain can be improved by ongoing and detailed mental awareness

---

[25] *The Brain's Way of Healing: Remarkable Discoveries and Recoveries From the Frontiers of Neuroplasticity* by Norman Doidge, MD (Penguin Group Viking, 2015)
[26] Ibid.

of movement. Improving the brains neuroplasticity also seems to involve interrupting the fight-or-flight response, and entering a calm state, in which thinking and reflection can take place. When this happens, chemical reactions are triggered that promote growth, conserve energy, and balance sleep cycles. Walking and entering a state of inner calm, while having a focused internal awareness of your movements – this sounds a lot like Ba Gua Circle Walking Nei Gong!

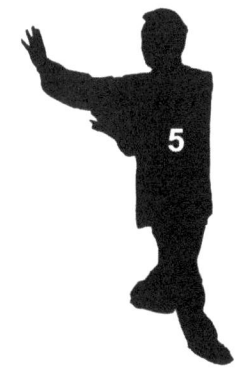

BA GUA ZHANG FOR EXERCISE & FITNESS

There are many ways in which people who practice Ba Gua Zhang benefit from the practice of circle walking. Circle walking promotes health, longevity, physical strength, stamina, coordination, and balance. Circle walking cultivates the *Qi*, calms the mind, improves mental concentration, and promotes unity of body and mind, while also teaching agile and effective self-defense skills. All of these aspects of physical, mental, and spiritual health can be improved simply through practicing circle walking. However walking the circle is only one part of Ba Gua Zhang:

- Ba Gua foundational training, aligns, loosens and opens up the joints and the energy pathways, while developing strength, balance, coordination endurance and resilience.

- Ba Gua Nei Gong removes blockages in the meridians and cultivates *Qi* and our ability to employ it in preserving health, generating power or healing others. Nei Gong practices like standing meditation or circle walking practice also teach us to sense inside the body.

- The forms and movements of Ba Gua flow from the Foundational Training and Nei Gong practices. They further develop the body's basic physical strength while also developing coordinated, efficient movements, speed and refined power (*Jin*). In addition, learning forms develops the ability to see and remember movement patterns.

- Ba Gua Zhang and its related Nei Gong exercises Neuro-muscularly reprogram the body to move efficiently and powerfully without tension or restriction.

- Partner exercises and self-defense application training acts as a kind of resistance training both physically, mentally and emotionally. This training exercise develops strength, and mental and emotional fortitude, while imparting practical self-defense skills. Partner work challenges our physical and mental adaptability to changing and even unpredictable circumstances. Practicing applications also engages the mind and body in the processes of creativity, discovery and experimentation.

- Rolling Hands, Pushing Hands and partnered circle walking drills refine one's sensitivity to exterior forces impinging on the body. In these practices, one senses or "listens" to the forces generated by the opponent/partner, so as to dissolve and redirect the incoming force. The listening ability developed in these practices has many applications to other physical activities and to our interactions with others.

- Weapons training builds strength and coordination through the manipulation of objects of varying size, shape and weight in space. This improves spatial awareness and the ability to extend our Mind-Intention and *Qi* outside of ourselves to the tip or striking surface of the weapon.

It is the combination of all of these aspects of the art of Ba Gua Zhang that produce a truly "fit" person. Using Ba Gua Zhang as an example, one begins to see that the Chinese view of health is global. Smooth, long muscles that can move completely through their natural range of motion are prized over bulky hypertrophied muscles. In traditional Chinese

Medicine, big, bulky muscles are thought to be a sign of local stagnation of *Qi* and blood. Flexibility is important, but not at the expense of joint stability. The ability to move naturally, in a coordinated, smooth and effortless way is more important than exerting oneself to the limit. Repeated over-exertion is thought to deplete the body's vital resources. A healthy person's meridians are clear and open. A healthy person displays intelligence, their mind is unclouded and their consciousness is bright and alert. Ba Gua Zhang redefines the goals of fitness into four aspects that can also be understood as stages of development:

1. Developing a healthy, strong body that is resistant to disease and a mind and nervous system that are relaxed and calm.

2. Stilling the activity of the mind in order to foster Spirit and intelligence.

3. The ability to maintain internal and external harmony and balance when confronted with external pressures and the challenges and vicissitudes of the world.

4. Harmony with the universal forces in the natural world.

The founder of Judo, Jigaro Kano, felt that the purpose of martial arts was to create a strong and healthy body, while simultaneously cultivating the mind and the spirit. Kano felt that well developed musculature was not a goal or something to be admired, but merely the foundation for development of the personality, mind and spirit. Almost a hundred years ago, he already saw that the development of Judo as a competitive spectator sport would be detrimental to the art.

Kano felt that the great benefit of martial arts like Judo and by extrapolation arts like Ba Gua Zhang was that they developed many different aspects of the mind and body:[27]

- Observation
- Memory
- Experimentation
- Imagination and Creativity
- Language
- Being Open-Minded
- Awareness

Observation

When practicing Ba Gua Zhang one observes both internally and externally. This dual awareness is important in sensing the energies and alignments of the body while also sensing what is happening outside. This is true whether one is working alone or with a partner. Part of training in martial arts is also improving one's ability to see movements and duplicate them, picking up the nuances and details that the teacher is manifesting. One also learns by observing other students, seeing what they do wrong and what they do right without judging or criticizing. Ba Gua Zhang practice improves our ability to see something, assimilate the important details, and duplicate it.

---

[27] *Mind over Muscle: Writings From the Founder of Judo*, compiled by Noaki Murata. Translated by Nancy H. Ross (Tokyo, New York, London: Kodansha International 2005).

Memory

Ba Gua Zhang has many movements and forms. Part of learning this art is learning to memorize and duplicate the movements and to remember the applications of the movements shown by the teacher. This aspect of training develops many aspects of the mind and cognition. Progress in this skill comes naturally if you can open yourself up to the process.

Imagination & Creativity

Imagination is an important aspect of Ba Gua Zhang, even in the basic training. In Nei Gong exercises, the practitioner tries to sense his or her connection with Heaven and Earth, and to imagine that it is possible to sense, and internally "see", the meridians and energy flows in the body. When learning the forms and movements, one imagines their possible applications and the opponent's logical responses. This is important, as the teacher cannot possibly teach all the applications and responses that might occur. He or she gives the student examples to stimulate the student's creativity and insight into the movements. Ba Gua Zhang also uses imagery from the *Yi Jing* and from the natural world. For example, what does "flowing like water" or "pouncing like a tiger" feel like? This requires imagination, thought and research on the part of the student.

Experimentation

As students learn movements and principles, ideas are generated. These ideas, whether they be in the realm of self-defense, or health and well being, must be examined and tested by experience. This process teaches one to adapt one's ideas and actions to the reality of the situation and to the circumstances. Discovery, experimentation, and adaptation bring growth.

Language

Language is an important part of learning anything and Ba Ga Zhang is no exception. Words have power. The teacher's explanations must be carefully thought out and the student must make sure that he or she understands the explanation clearly. Traditionally teachers spoke little, because putting something into words often fixes it in the listener's mind. Hence, the extensive use of imagery in the names and explanations of the movements. Imagery bypasses the conscious mind, allowing access to a deeper intuitive understanding.

Being Open-Minded

Ba Gua Zhang is an art that has many aspects and levels of practice. One must be open-minded to engage with the many facets of the art. Learning requires humility and "emptying one's cup" to embrace new ideas. This sometimes requires "investing in loss" – letting go of entrenched thinking or pre-conceived ideas. Being open-minded or "broad-minded" also means not being dogmatic or having over-confidence in your art or belief system, and not trying to impose those beliefs on others. In China broad-mindedness is recognized as important aspect of health. An exemplary person is said to have a Heart-Mind that is broad and open, while a small person is said to have a "narrow Heart-Mind" that is sullen and unhappy.

Masters of the internal arts believe that those who are adept at cultivating and nourishing Qi experience a unity of form, Qi and Spirit within themselves. Thus they attain a unity with the natural world, and in this process a natural spontaneity and compassion are developed. Internally in one's own body, this life-nourishing cultivation promotes longevity, while externally it strengthens resistance to disease, and promotes healthy relationships with others. Hence, practicing Ba Gua Zhang can eliminate illness, strengthen the body and allow one to live life to the fullest.

WHO CAN PRACTICE BA GUA ZHANG?

Ba Gua is suitable for many people of different ages. The discussion below can be useful to see if practicing the art of Ba Gua is a good fit for you and your life.

Children and Young Teenagers

Ba Gua and other Internal Arts are generally not suitable for children under the age of 15-16. Very young children do not need to consolidate energy in the body, but instead need to expend it in healthy pursuits. In China, many of the great masters I studied with, such as Li Gui Chong, Gao Ji Wu and Zhao Da Yuan, started martial arts at a young age, but they began with more external arts like *Chang Quan* (Long Fist), External Shaolin basic training, *Tan Tui* (Spring Legs), or *San Huang Pao Chui* (Three Emperor Cannon Fist). These arts strengthen the body with basic movements that improve flexibility, balance, and strength and emphasize the outward extension of energy. These arts are, to some degree, athletic and physically challenging in a direct and obvious way, but at the same time develop foundational skills that have a direct transfer to internal training. Later, at the age of 18-20, these masters moved on to study internal martial arts.

Some aspects of Ba Gua can be useful for younger teenagers to help them understand themselves in a time of growth, change and confusion. The ability to look inside, slow down and reside in internal and external stillness is valuable and can serve one in many aspects of life. Ba Gua's internal training can help young people to understand themselves, to think independently and reduce susceptibility to peer pressure. Awareness of oneself leads to awareness of others and the situation.

Older Teenagers and 20-Year Olds

Older teenagers often find that the internal arts are too slow and require too much patience. When I was 18, I tried Tai Ji Quan for a few months, but I could not stick with it. I did not have the patience for the slow process and slow precise movements. I soon took up Filipino martial arts (Eskrima/Kali) with its emphasis on weapons, fast fluid movements and immediate practicality for self-defense. In my late 20's I returned to the internal arts and found that internal training greatly improved my abilities in the Filipino arts, taking these arts to a higher level. Later I stopped practicing the Filipino martial arts in order to focus on the Xing Yi Quan and Ba Gua Zhang and traditional Chinese medicine.

Many teenagers and twenty-somethings have greater patience and maturity then I did and find something unique and enriching in the practice of Ba Gua Zhang. For some, Ba Gua Nei Gong helps them with mental focus, confidence and the ability to focus under stress. For others, it provides a unique philosophy for negotiating life. Regular practice helps build habits and self-discipline that can serve people in their twenties for the rest of their lives.

30-Year Olds

The 30's are often a difficult age for people to focus on a discipline like Ba Gua Zhang. In this period of one's life, the focus is often on building a career, marriage, raising children and extending one's life outward into the world. However, this is the perfect time to balance one's outward moving energy and focus with an inward looking practice that develops inner understanding, inner sensitivity, and inner calm. The practice of Ba Gua Zhang and Ba Gua Nei Gong also improves one's resistance to illness and builds the necessary reserve of energy to enjoy these years of work and expansion, while preventing exhaustion and depletion of one's physical, mental and emotional strength.

40-50 Year Olds

Zhang Hua Sen began training in Ba Gua Zhang in his forties. He felt this was an ideal time to begin Ba Gua training because one's life is settled and one has the time and mental focus to train. Master Zhang also observed that at this point in one's life one realizes that it is no longer possible to rely on one's natural strength, speed and athleticism. At this age, one is ready to relax and patiently nurture the internal refined power and speed that internal arts like Ba Gua Zhang develop. Although Zhang Hua Sen had previously studied martial arts and had endured the rigorous training necessary to perform martial roles in Perking Opera, he felt that his martial abilities matured after beginning to practice Ba Gua Zhang with Li Zi Ming.

**Zhang Hua Sen
and Li Zi Ming**

**Zhang Hua Sen
Teaching Tom Bisio
(Beijing, 1994)**

So if you are 40 or 50 years old don't think it is too late to begin studying Ba Gua or even become an advanced instructor in the art. Regular practice of Ba Gua can help the average 40 or 50 year old avoid unnecessary illness by promoting harmonious habits of body and mind.

60 Years Old and Up

Ba Gua Zhang is an ideal art and exercise for those over 60, who may be retired or working as intensely as ever. Ba Gua improves many qualities both physical and mental that tend to diminish with age unless they are carefully nurtured – balance, strength, reflexes, and mental engagement. Some of the measures of pre-mature aging are: reduced sense of balance and unsteadiness when walking or standing on one foot, decrease in bone density, decrease in muscle mass and strength, reduced flexibility in the spine and neck, and reduced lung capacity. Studies have shown that regular practice of arts like Ba Gua prevents these markers of aging.

One marker of early aging is Forward Head Syndrome, in which the head slowly moves forward, creating restricted head and neck movement, and the upper back becomes rounded, creating reduced movement in the scapula and rib cage. Forward Head Syndrome is now common in younger people who overuse computers, tablets and cell phones. The basic alignments and movements of Ba Gua teach you to maintain proper alignment and maintain suppleness in these areas. See the study on elderly Ba Gua practitioners below to learn more about what Ba Gua can do for your health and longevity.

The Chinese call Frozen Shoulder "50 Year Old Shoulder," because it affects older people who unknowingly reduce their natural movement due to restricted movement or injury. Once you stop lifting your arm overhead, it often becomes impossible to do so. When Master Wang Shi Tong taught me Ba Gua's unique method of using the Chinese saber, he mentioned that if you practice the saber form every day, you will never get frozen shoulder, because the movements of the saber form take the shoulder through all of its natural movements in a fluid smooth fashion that aids and strengthens joint function.

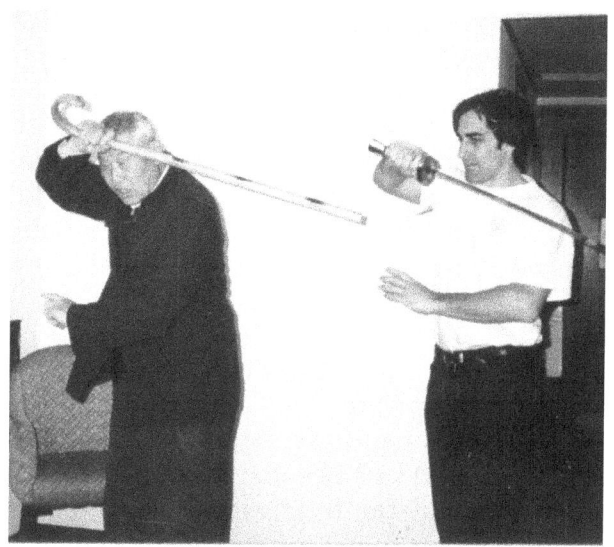

Wang Shi Tong Teaching Tom Bisio the Ba Gua Saber

As we age, balance becomes an important issue. There are several reasons for this:

1. As we age, cells in the vestibular system die off. The vestibular system is connected to centers in the brain that also control our balance. Loss of cells here effects how accurately we detect our position in space.

2. Our sight, the ability to focus and see things clearly, diminishes with age. So do depth perception, night vision and sensitivity to contrast. Eye problems also can impair, blur or distort vision. The loss of visual cues compromises balance.

3. Many people lose muscle mass and strength with age. Loss of muscle and strength affects one's ability to balance or restore equilibrium from a trip or slip

4. Usually one's reflexes and coordination diminish with age. Slower reflexes can make one more likely to stumble and slow corrective reaction.

5. Many people reduce their physical activity when they are older. There are many reasons for this. Often a minor injury leads one to favor a leg or an arm. This adaptation then becomes chronic, and throws off the body's innate integrity and proprioception, creating muscular imbalances that can affect balance.

The discussion above makes poor balance seem an inevitable consequence of aging, but Ba Gua practitioners in there seventies and eighties regularly exhibit excellent balance and perceptive faculties. Why? Because they have an embodied, daily practice that constantly engages vision, balance, inner and outer listening, proprioception, coordination and lower limb strength. Many students have found that Ba Gua's mud walking step is great way to negotiate the "black ice" that makes New York's sidewalks so treacherous in winter.

Master Gao Ji Wu, although already a formidable exponent of Ba Gua Zhang in his 50's, felt that he made a quantum leap in his Ba Gua after he retired at age 65, because he could now devote all of his energy to training, research and teaching. My own experience of approaching 60 is an increased sense of looking for an understanding of my place in the world and the trajectory of life that brought me to this point. Nei Gong and the meditative practices associated with Ba Gua Zhang, and the art's connections to the *Yi Jing* (Book of Changes), whose philosophy of understanding life as a state of constant change, are invaluable tools to moving smoothly through this phase of life.

Beijing Study of the Effects of Ba Gua on Health and Longevity

A recent study on the effects of Bag Gua on health and longevity compared 30 members of the Beijing Ba Gua Zhang Research Club, who all practiced. Ba Gua Zhang regularly and were at least 60 years old, with 30 subjects in the control group - retired workers of a wool factory, all in good health, who also took time to look after their health. Most of the retired factory workers walked daily and performed other light activities. A few of them practiced Tai Ji Quan, long distance running or cycling.

Under the same conditions, many medical and physiological measurements were taken from the subjects of both groups: X-rays of chest, lower back and hip, shoulder and vertebral column, range of motion, respiratory functions, cardiovascular functions, muscle working capacity, vision, audition, balance and limb circumference.The data obtained was divided into three groups: ages 60-69, over 70 years old and the total group data. The results:

1. Bone density tests revealed remarkable differences. Senile degeneration in bone was prevented or postponed by those people who regularly practiced Ba Gua Zhang and there was positive bone adaptation as a result of Ba Gua Zhang practice.

2. Observations on the vertebral column and hip joint range of motion, showed that because of frequent and wide movements of the lower back and hip in practicing Ba Gua Zhang, the range of motion of forward and lateral trunk flexion and lower back twisting of the those in the Ba Gua Group surpassed that of the Control Group

3. The respiratory functions of the Ba Gua Group significantly exceeded those of the Control Group. The differences between the two groups in vital capacity, maximal pulmonary ventilation, chest circumference, and difference between inhalation and exhalation were also significant. This is thought to be linked to the deep abdominal breathing that occurs when practicing Ba Gua Zhang.

4. No significant differences were found in heart rate or systolic pressure. Diastolic pressure of Ba Gua Group was lower than that of the Control Group.

5. Abnormal EKG was 20% lower in the Ba Gua Group, which showed that practicing Ba Gua Zhang has positive effects on cardiovascular function.

6. Working capacity of muscles often decreases with age and is an important index of senility. Hand gripping strength, forearm twisting force, endurance, and reaction time of the Ba Gua Group were far superior to these same markers in the Control Group, indicating the positive effects regular Ba Gua Zhang practice has on muscular strength, endurance and reaction time.

7. Balance (with eyes closed) was significantly better in the Ba Gua group.

8. Comparisons of the circumferences of upper arm, thigh and calf between the two groups showed a significant difference in favor of the Ba Gua group.[28]

---

28 *Medical and Physiological Observations of Old Men who Practice Ba Gua Zhang, by Gao Qiang*, Kang Ge Wu Xian Han Zhao and Chen Min Yi. (Beijing University of Physical Education. http://www.taichi-kungfu.com/classes/internal-kungfu/bagua-zhang-health-study/)

Ba Gua and Mental Health

One of the secrets of health and longevity espoused by Chinese centenarians is to live a regular life, with an established schedule. Having a regular practice of Ba Gua training that is performed at the same time everyday can have a large impact one one's health, not only because it establishes a regular exercise schedule, but because it also has positive effects on one's mental faculties and outlook on life. Emotional distress, depression and chronic stress have been linked to over-rumination. Physical training, which includes mindfulness and relaxed awareness of the whole body, dispels the tendency to dwell on one's thoughts and desires. In China this called "subduing the crazy monkey" and "catching the restless horse." "Crazy monkey" and "restless horse" refers to the heart and emotions jumping uncontrollably like a monkey, and the mind over-thinking and being mentally restless, like a restless horse. Ba Gua Zhang training forces you to attend to the moment, and this mental attitude is reinforced by a daily practice regimen.

I trained for a year and a half with Master Fu Shu Yun when she was in her late 70's. She could still touch her knee to her head with a straight leg kick, and perform all of her forms with vigor and martial spirit. Master Fu had trained at the Nanjing Central Kuoshu Academy in the 1930's when its faculty included some of the most famous internal martial artists of the time. In a 1991 interview Master Fu gave the following advice:

> *Now I do not practice martial arts so much. I know the forms so well that I cannot know them any better. I teach so much and get my exercise there. Now I only do my own sets of exercise each morning before I get out of bed. These exercises stretch every muscle and move every joint. Before I know it, two hours have passed. When I practice martial arts, I like to do it alone. That way it is more peaceful and quiet, and I can concentrate. I don't do meditation or Qi Gong – actually I*

never practiced Qi Gong Basically, I like peace and quiet. When I practice martial arts and do calligraphy, I find happiness and peace. I hate gossiping. It goes on a lot. Empty activities and gossip don't help you at all. Life is so easy without all that nonsense. Anyone who has good hobbies won't engage in empty activities. It is very important to have good hobbies.[29]

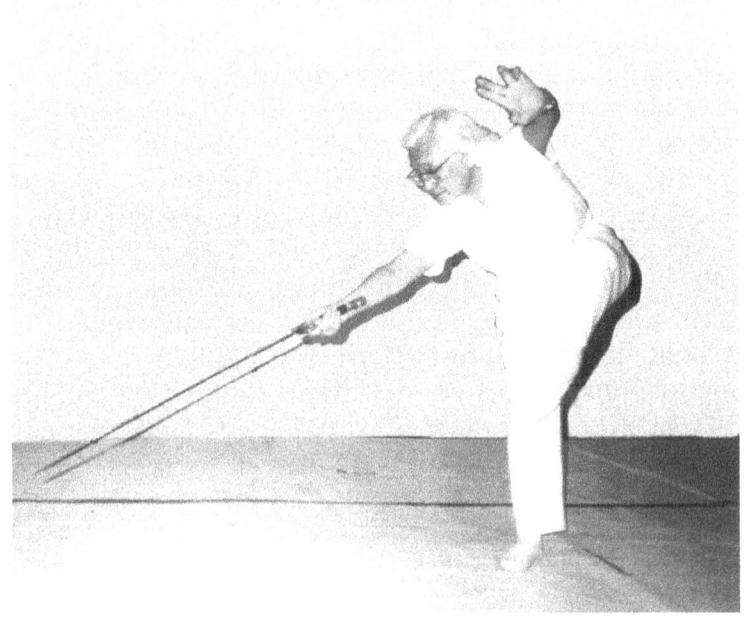

Master Fu Shu Yun in Action

Ba Gua for Office Workers

Ba Gua and its Nei Gong practices are especially valuable for those who work in an office and are largely sedentary throughout the day. The dangers of sitting too much are becoming more known as large percentages of the population spend more time on the Internet and computers.

---

[29] *An Interview with Fu Shu Yun,* (Qi Magazine: Journal of Health and Fitness. Winter 1991, Vol.1 No.4).

Researchers in Toronto looked at 47 studies examining the relationship between sitting and mortality, according to the findings, published last week in the journal *Annals of Internal Medicine*. They found that people who sat for long periods were more likely to suffer from health problems than people who sat less. This includes higher risk of breast cancer, colon ands colorectal problems, endometrial and ovarian cancers, heart problems and diabetes. Researchers also found that the people who exercised generally faced lower risks of these health conditions than those who didn't exercise. But exercising did not completely counteract the risks that came with sitting for a long time.[30]

Other problems related to prolonged sitting:

- Prolonged sitting causes foggy thinking as the brain gets less oxygen when you are sedentary for too long.

- It's common to hold your neck and head forward while working at a computer or cradling a phone to your ear. This puts strain on the cervical vertebrae causing muscular imbalance, which can lead to neck pain, sore shoulders and back pain.

- Sitting puts more pressure on your spine than standing, and the toll on your back health is even worse if you're sitting hunched in front of a computer. It's estimated that 40 percent of people with back pain have spent long hours at their computer each day. When you sit, the spinal disks are compressed and receive less circulation, causing them to lose flexibility over time.

---

[30] *Too Much Sitting May Have Some Serious Health Effects - Even If You Exercise.* (Washington Post: https://www.washingtonpost.com/national/health-science/too-much-sitting-may-have-some-serious-health-effects--even-if-you-exercise/2015/01/26/d0345a4a-a250-11e4-b146-577832eafcb4_story.html)

- Sitting slackens and weakens your abdominal muscles and gluteal muscles, but tightens up your hips and psoas muscles. Over time this can cause hip problems and reduced balance.

- Prolonged sitting leads to poor circulation in the legs, which can cause cold feet, varicose veins, and blood clots.

The postural alignments in used in Ba Gua Zang, combined with the deep abdominal breathing and relaxed internal focus go a long way toward undoing the effects of prolonged sitting. The Mud Walking Step used in Circle Walking Nei Gong corrects many of the postural misalignments mentioned above, and the following differences can be felt in less the 10 minutes of practice:

- Improved circulation

- Energized brain and nervous system

- Relaxed shoulders, neck and back

- Improvement in vision

- Immediate sense of well-being and relaxation

If you don't have room to walk a circle, or you are self-conscious about doing that kind of exercise on front of your associates, the standing mediation exercises, Patting Exercises and *Qi* Cultivation Exercise that are part of the Ba Gua Foundational training can also produce these kinds of results in a short time. These practices can be done in a small office or a cubicle. After doing these exercises, take a short walk, even if is just down the hall, and save the circle walking practice for after work, or your lunch break.

People who multi-task often think they get more done than those who methodically get a job done and move onto the next. Numerous studies have shown that this is not the case.

Practicing Ba Gua Zhang and Nei Gong teaches you to sense and attend your internal environment while being aware of the external environment. This is not multi-tasking, but creates a unified, integrated awareness that helps you to complete work and organize your thoughts more coherently. Taking a break to practice Nei Gong or Ba Gua will increase rather than interfere with your productivity.

If you are completely relaxed and stress-free, your mind can work more effectively. The right side of your brain, which is responsible for creating new ideas, is more active when engaged in practices like Ba Gua, Nei Gong and standing or seated meditation, in which one lets distracting thoughts disperse and engages a relaxed internal focus. As a result:

- The body and mind feel recharged

- Memory and mental focus improve

- Blood circulation to the brain increases

- Creativity is enhanced

David Levy, a computer scientist and professor with the Information School at the University of Washington, found that those who had meditation training were able to stay on a task longer and were less distracted. Levy and his co-authors discovered that meditation also improved test subjects' memory, while easing their stress.

One group of managers underwent eight weeks of mindfulness-based meditation training. A second group received eight weeks of body-relaxation training. The third group received no training, but then was given the same training as the first group after eight weeks. Each group was given a stressful test before and after the eight-week period. The test involved task switching, and tasks that required accuracy, and included using calendars, instant messaging, phones and word-processing tools to perform common office duties. Stress level and memory performance while performing tasks was also assessed. The meditation group had lower stress levels and could concentrate longer without distraction. For the other two groups this was not the case, but the third group who had received no training found that these same improvements occurred after they were later given mindfulness training.[31]

Ba Gua for Health Care Practitioners

As a professional practitioner of traditional Chinese medicine for over 25 years, I can say without hesitation that the most important part of my ability to effectively treat patients was training in internal martial arts. I began my study of Chinese medicine by learning Gong Fu *Die Da* (Trauma) Medicine, *Tui Na* (Medical Massage) and Bone Setting (*Zheng Gu*), as an extension of the martial arts training. Later I went on to formally study acupuncture and Chinese herbal medicine.

The practice of Ba Gua Zhang and Nei Gong inculcates correct and aligned movement patterns in the body on both a conscious and unconscious level. This has many implications for health practitioners. If you are performing massage or physical medicine, working in proper posture and alignment prevents you from injuring yourself, because you are using the body in a way that protects you own joints and tissue. Although one can intellectually understand correct alignment and may even counsel patients on posture, without a regular embodied practice that incorporates correct body mechanics, posture and alignment quickly fall by the wayside as one is attending to the client or patient.

---

[31] *Meditation can Keep You More Focused at Work*, by Anita Bruzzese. (USA Today:satoday30.usatoday.com/money/jobcenter/workplace/bruzzese/story/201 2-07-08/meditation-helps-your-work/56071024/1)

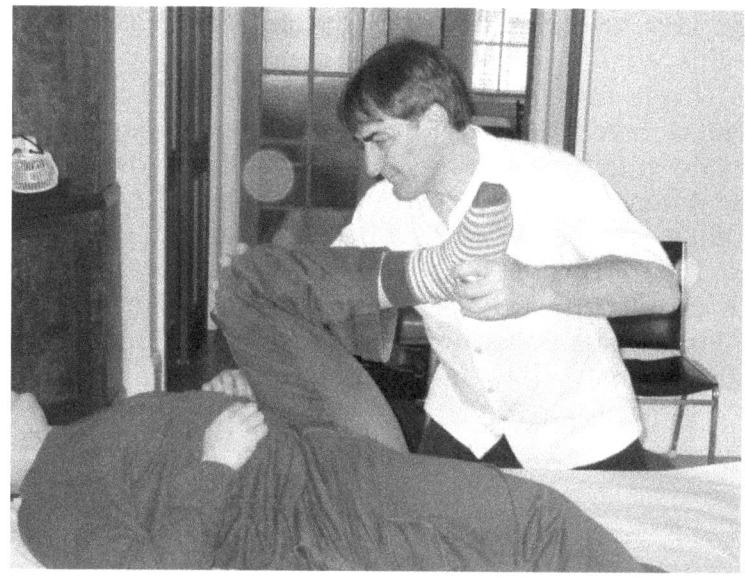

Tui Na Mobilization Technique

Many massage therapists use their hands incorrectly, in a fashion that is disconnected from the body, and therefore end up injuring their hands and wrists. In Ba Gua Zhang, the postures and movements create an integrated structural alignment that is dynamic and ongoing. It quickly becomes second nature, and the body automatically applies these principles to other activities.

When the body is aligned and connected internally and externally, it is relaxed. *Qi* does not smoothly flow through tense muscles, or through joints that are bent at angles that reduce the pliability of the limb or body area. This is much like a hose. If the hose is kinked, bent or blocked, water does not flow properly through it. When *Qi* flows smoothly, we can achieve more with less effort. For a massage therapist this can mean using less isolated muscular force to achieve the desired result. For the physician, it can lead to increased alertness and the ability to make diagnostic connections that go beyond the obvious.

When you are aligned with the internal *Qi* is flowing smoothly, you have an increased awareness of your internal state. This in turn increases awareness of subtle cues that the patient is revealing. It allows these cues to penetrate and percolate into one's consciousness without over-thinking them. When you are aligned and the internal *Qi* is flowing smoothly, your sense of touch becomes refined. For example, when I perform *Tui Na* (Chinese Medical Massage), my hands can penetrate deeper and more quickly into the tissue than my assistants because I can feel the subtle changes in the tissue that allow me to enter and engage with the person's energy.

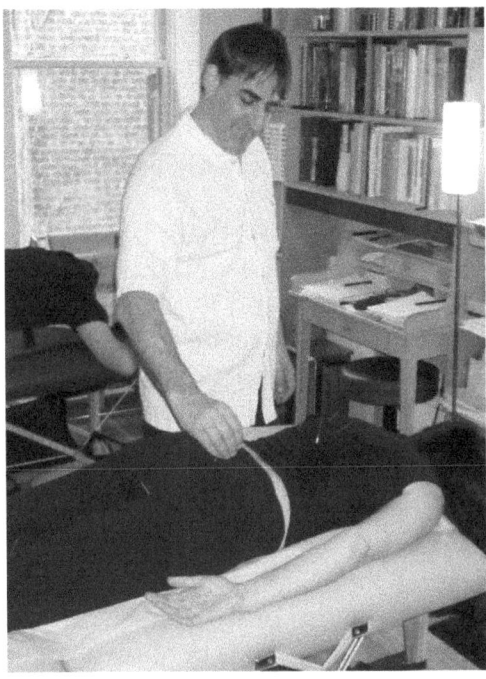

Acupuncture in the Clinic

These same factors also improve one's ability to read the pulse, insert and manipulate acupuncture needles more smoothly, and sense the internal changes occurring in the patient's body through the handle of the needle.

Ba Gua Zhang develops the ability to focus with a relaxed, but vigilant awareness. This is a useful ability to have, especially when one works in a busy clinic treating many people each day.

One aspect of Oriental medicine really stands out in comparison with Western medicine: the idea that the practitioner should be aligned, centered and healthy and should lead a harmonious lifestyle. This medical philosophy does not mean that practitioners of Oriental medicine do not get sick. It does mean that they tend to address health problems before they manifest into something serious and that they adjust their lifestyle in accordance with the seasons and environment in order to prevent disease or at least recover more quickly. This idea also underscores another difference: Chinese physicians attempt to understand, on a visceral level, how a healthy body at optimal functioning operates. This understanding is not cerebral knowledge, but knowledge that comes from the daily practice of disciplines like Nei Gong, Ba Gua Zhang and Tai Ji Quan. The physician must internally have a sense of what aligned joints, relaxed movement, and open, unblocked meridians feel like. Only then it is possible to really understand what the opposite situation feels like when touching a patient. This kind of knowledge cannot be learned from a book, it comes from within (from the "bones"), and is rooted in practice and experience.

A sense of whole body integrity and correct posture and alignment are facets of internal awareness that help to prevent injury and make one aware of subtle changes in the body's status quo. Disease starts with small imbalances or disruptions in the flow of energy. Detected early, these things are easily rectified. With late detection, the problem can be more entrenched and more difficult to treat. Teaching patients Ba Gua Nei Gong exercises helps them to take better care of themselves, and makes them realize that they are in control of their own health and can prevent illness and injury through correct exercise and a common sense approach to life. This is true preventative medicine.

I often prescribe Ba Gua exercises for patients with musculo-skeletal problems, because they reconnect injured areas to the *Dantian* and *Mingmen* and restore whole body integrity. My associates and I regularly prescribe a simplified version of Ba Gua Circle Walking Nei Gong, called the "Slow Walk," for hip knee and ankle problems, because this exercise restores balance to the leg muscles and integrates the action of the lower limb with the upper body and the *Dantian.*

Lastly, regular practice of Ba Gua Zhang and Nei Gong helps to prevent fatigue and burnout. Listening to complaints and problems day after day, without re-invigorating oneself is often what leads to burnout. Internal practices such as Ba Gua Zhang and Nei Gong act like a fountain of energy which enlivens, sustains and nourishes the practitioner physically, emotionally and even spiritually, allowing him or her to constantly draw on the best within themselves.

Athletes and Martial Arts Practitioners

Many athletes have benefited from practicing Ba Gua Zhang and Nei Gong. Cross training in internal arts has been shown to improve various aspects of athletic performance There are endless examples of athletes who have improved their oxygen update, lung capacity an endurance through the deep "Kidney" breathing that is fundamental to these practices. Kidney breathing also helps manage the mind and emotions during competition.

The ability to sense the *Dantian/Mingmen*, the internal center of gravity and the hub around which movement revolves, is invaluable for all sports. Letting movement emanate from the waist improves power, balance and fluidity of motion, while Circle Walking Nei Gong improves the balance and stability of the lower limbs. Several golfers reported improved performance after practicing the *Tian Gan* ("Heavenly Stem") Exercises, which work with shifting weight and twisting, torsional power emanating from the spine. They also found that the *Tian Gan* exercises corrected some of the muscular imbalances created by golf, an activity that is inherently imbalanced by the one-sided swinging action.

Ba Gua Zhang helps prevent joint, muscle and spine injuries by creating correct internal and external alignments and mechanics. This can help extend one's athletic career. Additionally Ba Gua training accelerates healing, while retraining the proprioception that is often lost with an injury. This gets athletes back in the game sooner and prevents re-injury.

Over the years I have had many martial artists from other styles try Ba Gua. Some studied only a few months, others stayed for a year or more, and some gave up their previous style and switched to Ba Gua Zhang. All of them reported improvements in their ability. One highly skilled martial artist, proficient in many styles reported more effortless power delivery. He surprised sparring partners and himself by striking them from a short distance and throwing them back several feet. One professional Thai boxer adopted some of Ba Gua's tactics into his fighting style and this has also been true with Filipino martial artists and Brazilian Jiu Jitsu practitioners.

My own experience with this came when I was teaching and competing in Filipino martial arts, while studying Xing Yi and Ba Gua. My Xing Yi and Ba Gua skills were rudimentary to say the least, but my training partners in Filipino arts commented that "something" had changed. They said I was hitting harder and faster and when we closed to close quarters they had trouble moving me. I attribute this to the foundational training I was doing in the internal arts.

It is not uncommon for athletes and dancers to say that they find Nei Gong and the internal arts boring and the movements too slow. This is usually because they like to move freely and find the Foundational Level of internal arts training too regimented. This is a basic misunderstanding of the traditional way of learning, where one can be creative and "free" after rigorous mastery of the basics. Building on the experience of past masters rather than "re-inventing the wheel" saves valuable time and accelerates one's ability to be truly creative. The second misunderstanding is that this perception tends to look at the internal arts from an external point of view. The goal in internal arts like Ba Gua Zhang is not to show what is happening externally, but to experience spontaneous movement internally. In Ba Gua Zhang, even when you are standing still externally, on the inside continuous movement, change and transformation dynamically unfold. By shifting the paradigm from being creative and strong externally to sensing and observing the unending changes and transformations (the choreography) occurring internally, athletes and dancers can gain a better appreciation of the art of Ba Gua Zhang,

WHAT IS AN INTERNAL MARTIAL ART?

Internal Martial arts are collectively referred to as the *Nei Jia Quan*. *Nei Jia Quan*(內家拳) literally means "inner family boxing" or "inner school boxing." This term refers specifically to styles of martial arts that in English we call "internal." Today these styles are considered to include Tai Ji Quan, Xing Yi Quan, Ba Gua Zhang, Tong Bei Quan, Yi Quan (Da Cheng Quan) and Liu He Ba Fa. Other styles are sometimes called "internal," including the Japanese art of Aikido. However, as the term *Nei Jia* is a Chinese concept, we must examine define and examine the *Nei Jia* in the context of Chinese martial arts. In fact, many teachers of internal martial arts never really say what an internal art is. This is because the nature of something internal is that it is sensed and experienced internally rather than perceived externally. Hence words are poor conveyers of what the concept "internal" actually means.

Triads

In this discussion, the idea of triads – groups of three – will be used to help understand the concept of internal. Triads are an important concept in Chinese thought. The most basic triad in Chinese philosophy is that of Heaven, Earth and Human Beings. This is most often depicted with Heaven above, Earth below and Human Beings in the center. This triad is the basis of *San Ti Shi,* the "Trinity" posture, or Three Body Pattern in Ba Gua Zhang and Xing Yi Quan (Form-Intention or Form-Image Boxing). From this triad, many other triads have been developed to explain internal arts and internal training. Heaven's energy (Yang *Qi*) flows downward and is received by Earth. Earth's energy (Yin *Qi*) flows upward. The two interact and co-mingle in living things. Earth manifests and upholds physical forms in response to Heaven's images. This creates an interaction of form and intention, images and manifestations, *Qi* and substance.

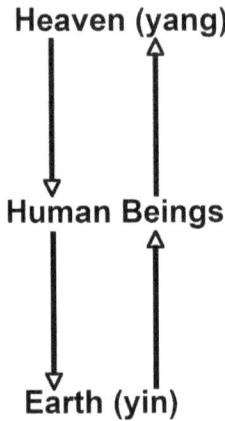

Internal and External Martial Arts

The differences between internal and external martial arts can be subtle. Comparisons are complicated by the fact that many "external" martial arts also employ some internal training methods and many "internal" martial arts also have external training methods. At the top of the mountain the view is the same for everyone. When individuals have attained a high level of skill in martial arts they have similar characteristics and abilities regardless of style or method. The difference is, to some degree, in the path chosen to climb the mountain. Every path has it pitfalls, benefits, sidetracks and provides different points of view. Even for practitioners of the same style, the individual path to the summit will vary based upon a multitude of factors: life experience, physical wherewithal, training partners, mental and emotional outlook, etc. In the 1980's I trained in the Philippines with Filemon "Momoy" Canete, an expert in

Filipino martial arts, whose specialty was *Espada y Daga* (stick and dagger fighting). At that point Master Canete was in his 80's and he exhibited many of the characteristics one associates with internal arts masters: relaxed effortless power, exquisite sensitivity and timing, the ability to heal through touch and prayer and a clear and vibrant spirit. In the picture below his spear thrust is imbued with power, intention and spirit.

Filemon "Momoy" Canete

Yet Master Canete's art would be classified as external, because his method for reaching this high level of ability focused on the external body and techniques and did not seem to have a language to talk about the subtleties of internal energy, body alignment, breath, and internal connection, even though he so clearly manifested all of these things. My observation was that many of his senior students approximated his obvious "external" skills, but not his "internal" ones.

At first glance, the primary difference between internal and external martial arts seems to be one of method. Speaking generally, the focus of internal arts is on principles, rather than specific techniques. Internal arts have techniques, but from the very beginning it is understood that techniques are merely expressions of the principles, and that the ultimate goal is to create techniques in the moment out of the interaction of one's energy and intention with the opponent's energy and intention. Secondly, while generally speaking the external arts focus their training methods on developing muscular strength, speed and athletic prowess, internal arts stress relaxation, mind-intention, stillness and natural movement. Thirdly, the internal arts use alignment, breath and structural dynamics to actualize the movement of the vital force (*Qi*) through the channels and collaterals (*Jing Luo*) or meridians. This is said to cultivate "whole body power" which does not rely on muscular strength, speed and athleticism. This idea has considerable overlap with the idea of body mechanics – i.e.: biomechanical principles of movement that increase efficiency. However, the two concepts are not identical.

Internal	**External**
Principles	Techniques
Relaxation; Mind-Intention	Muscular Strength; Speed
Alignment; Breath; Structure	Athleticism; Biomechanics

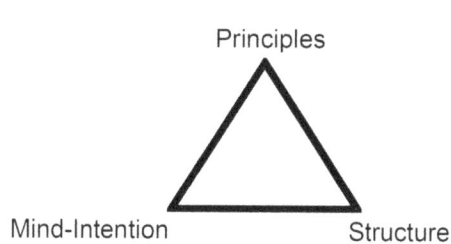

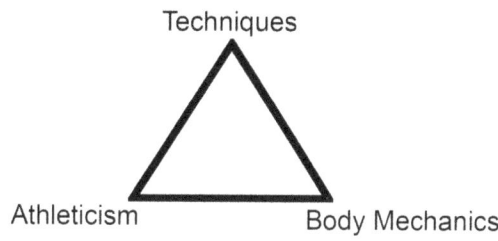

Lastly, and perhaps most importantly, the internal arts have a language to talk about the aspects mentioned above that we are calling "internal," and a effective training method that inculcates these principles. Hence training in internal martial arts requires that one understand the language and terminology and follow the method.

Internal and External Exercise

One interesting way to look at these differentiations is by examining the concept of the "Three Harms" in the practice of Nei Gong. The three harms provide an excellent differentiation between "internal" exercise and "external" exercise. The three harms are:

1. Forced Breathing

Forced Breathing can cause a stuffy, distended feeling in the chest and diaphragm. Forced breathing can also damage the Lung *Qi*. Breathing should be free, natural and unrestrained.

2. Labored Use of Strength

Holding tension or power in a single part of the body in order to exert force. Not only does forced tension break the feeling of connected, whole body movement, it also leads to stagnation of *Qi* and blood in local areas.

3. Throwing Out the Chest & Sucking In the Abdomen

Throwing out the chest and drawing in the abdomen can lead to stasis of *Qi* in the chest, so that the *Qi* fails to descend to *Dantian*. The *Qi* floats upward, the balance of the body is thrown off, and energy is blocks and cannot flow through the whole body.

It is easy to see that the forced breath, panting and chest breathing that is a result of forcing the heart to work harder, as in aerobics and calisthenics, is the opposite of the breathing in Nei Gong exercises, in which the breathing occurs deep in the diaphragm ("Kidney Breathing"), and is slow, soft, long and even. Weight training and calisthenics, which isolate muscle groups so that they can be worked to the maximum, or even to "failure," involve the labored use of strength, as opposed to the whole-body connected movement favored in internal exercise. Lastly, the over-developed chest and shoulders and washboard flat stomach, favored by athletes and proponents of external exercise, is the antithesis of the relaxed chest and shoulders and rounded belly that result from performing internal exercises.

The Six Harmonies

Another pair of triads that internal martial arts practitioners often use to differentiate internal from external are the Six Harmonies – three internal and three external. The six harmonies discuss principles that are fundamental to internal exercise and internal martial arts.

Three External Harmonies

Harmony between Shoulder and Hip

Harmony between Elbow and Knee

Harmony between Hand and Foot

Three Internal Harmonies

Harmony between Mind and Intention (*Yi*)

Harmony between Intention (*Yi*) and *Qi*

Harmony between *Qi* and Power/Force (*Jin Li*)

In the internal martial arts, the shoulder and hip move together and support each other, as do the elbow and knee, and hand and foot. These connections mean that these joints are linked and line up for efficient structure and power delivery. The shoulder is considered to be the "root" of the arm, the elbow is the "middle" and the hand is the "tip". Similarly, the hip is the root, the knee is the middle and the foot is the tip. Power and force come from the root and manifest in the tip. In substance this dynamic is the same – or should be – in both internal and external exercise and internal and external martial arts. To some degree it is just a question of correct body mechanics.

The Internal Harmonies are a different matter. They must link with the three External Harmonies in a seamless way.

The Mind-Intention (*Yi*) guides the *Qi*, which in turn actualizes force and power, which are themselves an expression of the mind and intention. This is not as simple as deciding to do something with force and then doing it. *Zhan Zhuang* or "stake standing" is a good example. Standing or holding fixed postures is one of the fundamental exercises in internal martial arts. In holding the embrace posture for example, the body relaxes, and the joints are aligned (external harmonies). As one stands, the intention guides the *Qi* to the tips of the body so that *Qi* fills the entire body. At the same time, there are oppositional forces operating in every direction which are not a product of bone, muscle and sinew but of the intention: The head and upper back erect upward while the tail sinks down, producing oppositional forces that pull the spine in opposite directions. The arms feel like they are supporting and embracing inward, while at the same time the arms are pulling apart. Simultaneously, throughout the body, there is twisting, spiraling, wrapping inward and outward, extending and stretching, retracting, embracing, pulling apart and pushing together. These forces are manifestations of Yin and Yang, positive and negative – they are oppositional but also complimentary. When these forces are balanced, body tension is minimized. All of this is a product of internal intention and internal "movement," occurring without visible (external) muscle tension or movement.

Additionally, in holding postures or body patterns, whether they are *San Ti Shi* (in Xing Yi) or *Ding Shi* (in Ba Gua Zhang), there is an internal sensing going on. The oppositional and yet complimentary forces, allow one to sense the stillness within movement and the movement within stillness. Two equal and opposing forces produce no visible movement – they allow one to sense stillness. Yet within this stillness the forces are still operating – there is movement inside. As the body relaxes into the postures, one feels comfortable and at ease, the muscles relax and the bones seem to support the body, while the muscles slacken and let go. Within this relaxation, this slackening, there is still force and strength, the product of the oppositional forces. Within the strength there is relaxation and flexibility. The body is not committed in any one direction; it is moving in all directions at the same time. Even though the body may feel still, and appears to be still, there is a faint stirring of movement that is constantly in the process of being actualized.

The Concept of Qi

Qi is a concept integral to the internal harmonies and to the oppositional forces discussed above. But what is *Qi*? There is no single word in the English language that adequately expresses the concept of *Qi*. It can be translated to mean a gas or a vapor, or understood as electromagnetic waves or fields of force. The famous Chinese scholar Joseph Needham felt that the term: "Matter-Energy" might most appropriately express the idea of *Qi*.[32] For simplicity, *Qi* is often erroneously referred to as "Energy" or "Vital-Energy" in medical discussions. Webster's Dictionary defines "Energy" as follows:

- Vitality or affective force
- The capacity of acting, operating or producing an effect
- Inherent power
- Vigorousness
- Activity and the product or effect of activity
- The capacity for doing work or the equivalent, as in a coiled spring (potential energy) or a speeding train

---

[32] *The Shorter Science & Civilization in China: Vol 1, by* Joseph Needham, (Cambridge University Press, 1978) p.239.

- Having existence independent of matter (as light or X-rays traversing a vacuum)[33]

Qi is at the same time all and none of these things. To understand the concept of *Qi* more clearly, it is helpful to study the ideogram itself and to look at how the Chinese have conceptualized *Qi* throughout the centuries. The Chinese character for Qi depicts vapors curling and rising from the ground to form clouds above. The ancient oracle bone, bronze or seal form of the character depicts this very clearly:

Qi

Later the ideogram was expressed showing vapors rising to form a layer of clouds. This is also part of the character for steam:

Qi   气

Later still, the grain radical was added to the character: *mi* (rice) which is depicted as: 米. This creates an image of steam or vapor rising from cooking rice.

气 + 米 = 氣 Qi

Today, the modern simplified character is once again: 气.

Various interpretations may be made. The ideogram for *Qi* may depict the nurturing energies of rice reduced to their smallest component, a vapor, or as Needham indicated, the changing states of energy and matter.

---

[33] *Webster's 3rd New International Dictionary,* Springfield, Mass.: G &C: Merriman Co., 1961, p.751.

In early Chinese Texts, *Qi* is used to refer to various phenomena:

- Air
- Mists and Fog
- Moving Clouds
- Aromas
- Vapors
- Smoke
- Breathing – Inhalation and Exhalation

In common usage, *Qi* can refer to air, gases and vapors, smells, spirit, vigor, morale, attitude, the emotions (particularly anger), as well as tone, atmospheric changes, the weather, breath and respiration. In the body *Qi* is often discerned by its actions, *the balanced and orderly vitalities partly derived from the air we breathe, that cause physical changes and maintain life.*[34] In Chinese medicine, when we say that someone is healthy, it is because the functioning of their body, the physical manifestations of their *Qi*, are orderly and without dysfunction. Every movement, every thought and emotion, our metabolism, every movement of life and consciousness, is in some measure a manifestation of *Qi*. Benjamin Schwartz adds an important element to the definition of *Qi* when he says:

> *It is also clear however, that Qi comes to embrace properties, which we would call psychic, emotional, spiritual, numinous and even "mystical." It is precisely at this point that Western definitions of "matter" and the*

---

[34] *Traditional Medicine in Contemporary China: Science, Medicine and Technology in East Asia Vol. 2*, by Nathan Sivin. (Ann Arbor: Center for Chinese Studies University of Michigan, 1987) p. 46-7.

physical, which systemically exclude these properties from their definition, do not at all correspond to Qi.[35]

Qi and Martial Arts

In relationship to the martial arts, the concept of *Qi* has to be looked at in connection with the Six Harmonies, which describe the internal and external connection and body alignments necessary to produce connected, agile movement and refined whole-body power. This connection certainly involves the breath ("*Qi* of Heaven"), which brings in the oxygen that not only keeps us alive, but is also necessary for a host of body functions. Respiration oxygenates the blood and expels waste products like carbon dioxide. At a cellular level, oxygen is the indispensable key that unlocks the stored energy of ATP. The breaking of ATP's chemical bonds provides the energy for mechanical work, electrical impulses, cell division secretion, etc. Sheldon Paul Hendler MD, stresses the importance of ATP:

> *Without ATP there is no energy, no life. It is ATP that we utilize to act, feel, think. It provides the energy we use every time we "fire" a brain cell, contract a muscle, repair a cell, and reproduce our kind. Not surprisingly it takes a lot of ATP to make all of this happen if you are active physically, you are making/using an amount of ATP close to your ideal body weight each day. The body and brain are sensitive to even very small reductions in ATP production. This sensitivity is expressed in terms of aches and pains, confusion, intermittent fatigue and greater susceptibility to infection, and finally, chronic fatigue and persistent illness.[36]*

Dr. Hendler suggests that improper breathing can actually result in progressive damage to the heart through the

---

[35] *The World of Thought in Ancient China* by Benjamin I. Schwartz (Cambridge, Mass: The Belknap press of Harvard University Press, 1985) p. 181.
[36] *The Oxygen Breakthrough: 30 Days to an Illness-Free Life* by Sheldon Saul Hendler, MD, PhD (Pocket Books, 1990) p.19-20.

cumulative effect of small, but repeated arterial spasms. Dr, Hendler advocates maximizing oxygen flow and ATP production through the very same basic breathing exercise that forms the foundation of internal martial arts training – Kidney Breathing (*Dantian* Breathing)

Breathing, and particularly *Dantian* or "Kidney Breathing" and its variations used in internal martial arts, also creates a pressure dynamic in the lower abdomen and low back that is constantly gathering and releasing, like a spring coiling and uncoiling. *Qi* and Breath are intimately connected, yet *Qi* is also said to flow through the meridians. As Tai Ji expert Mike Sigman points out, the Sinew Channels or Tendino-Muscular Meridians, which are intimately bound up with the fascial network of the body, are likely the mechanism by which *Qi* and Power are intimately connected. The fascial network represents one integrated continuum that goes from the internal cranial reciprocal tension membranes to the plantar fascia of the feet. Helene Langevin, PhD, a research scientist working at the University of Vermont and her colleagues have done research that suggests an overlap between the fascia and the channels and collaterals. Langevin and others speculate that the connective tissue network is a "sophisticated communication system of yet unknown potential:

> *'Loose' connective tissue forms a network extending throughout the body including subcutaneous and interstitial connective tissues. The existence of a cellular network of fibroblasts within loose connective tissue may have considerable significance as it may support yet unknown body-wide cellular signaling systems. ...Our findings indicate that soft tissue fibroblasts form an extensively interconnected cellular network, suggesting they may have important, and so*

far unsuspected integrative functions at the level of the whole body.[37]

Modern science has also found that connective tissue and cells have a quasi-crystalline structure and to some degree, behave like crystals. The regularity of structure of this tissue enhances its ability to conduct, process and store energy and information. The solid-state properties of connective tissue may produce its apparently cooperative and collective phenomena. There is every indication that connective tissue generates electricity when compressed, creating a piezoelectric effect. Some scientists feel that the piezoelectric signals generated by connective tissue form an essential and vast biological communication system.[38]

The Sinew Channels "knot" (wrap around) at the joints, encasing them and wrapping them so that the joints have integrity and can generate physical force. The nexus of these forces is in the *Dantian* and *Mingmen,* which lie inside the lower abdomen and lower back. Here, the pressure of the breath combines with the Sinew Channels and the bow-like structures of the spine and limbs to generate fundamental movements that are akin to fetal movement: opening, closing, extending, contracting, spiraling rightward and leftward. From these fundamental movements all other movements are created.

The "*Qi* of Earth" is found in the connection of our body with the ground. The *Dantian, Mingmen* and their connection with the lower limbs are the foundation for movement and the release of power. Without a stable foundation, power cannot be released and the body cannot move quickly and with agility. As Archimedes said: "Give me a firm place to stand, and a lever long enough, and I will move the world. "

---

[37] *The Amazing Fascial Web Part 1* by Leon Chaitow, ND, DO (*Massage Today*, May 2005, Vol. 5, Issue 5).
[38] *A Biophysical Basis for Acupuncture* by James L. Oscherman Ph.D. (Dover, NH: Nature's Own Research Association, 1993) p.19-23.

This statement implies that in order to employ strength or power, one needs a stable platform. If the place you stand (the fulcrum) is unstable, then power will not be properly transmitted and will come back against your own body. Therefore, the fulcrum (point of support) is very important. The body's fulcrum is the feet. If the feet are not stable (for example: standing on ice), it is difficult to release power.

In the internal martial arts, *Qi* and breath are said to gather in *Dantian* while the body relaxes and sinks. *It is said that "gathering power is like pressing a spring." Where is the Spring Pressed? In Dantian. What is the spring? Your internal Qi. When the whole body is relaxed, the internal Qi is gathered and pressed firmly in Dantian. Guide Qi with Intention and promote Li [power] with Qi, section by section, so that it can instantly burst outward from Dantian along the meridians and through the bones.*[39] One uses the breath to relax the muscles and tissues while making sure the limbs are slightly bent or curved. Then the accumulated internal *Qi* (and potentiated power) is compressed like a spring and the relaxed muscles lengthen like a bowstring that is stretched and ready to shoot. *Qi* is then released and goes outward. Movement and power must initiated by *Dantian* and *Mingmen* rather than by the limbs, otherwise there is no connection to the body's foundation and power will not be rooted.

Dantian

The *Dantian* is often described as being 1.5-3 inches below the navel, or it is associated with the acu-point *Qihai* (Ren 6 – "Sea of Qi"), and with *Mingmen* ("Life Gate" – Du 4). In fact the Dantian is really an interconnection of the energies of *Qihai* and *Mingmen* that is inside the body, rather than on the surface. Some people refer to this "ball-like" pivotal area as the Middle *Dantian* (see the diagram on the next page).

---

[39] *Practical Qin Na Part 1: Explanation of the Qin Na Nine Heaven Secret Text,* by Zhao Da Yuan, translation by Huang Guo Qi and Tom Bisio. Edited by Tom Bisio (Denver: Outskirts Press, 2015) p. 261.

When people talk about *Dantian,* they are usually referring to this Middle *Dantian.* However on another level, a *Dantian* is a place where energy gathers and is transformed or transmuted. Therefore in martial arts, Nei Gong, meditation and Daoism we often speak of an upper, middle or lower *Dantian.* In this paradigm, the lower *Dantian* becomes the "Middle Dantian" mentioned above,and is largely associated with the *Jing* (Essence), the Middle *Dantian* moves to the chest and is associated with breath and *Qi,* and the upper *Dantian* is in the head and brain and is associated with the *Shen* (Spirit).

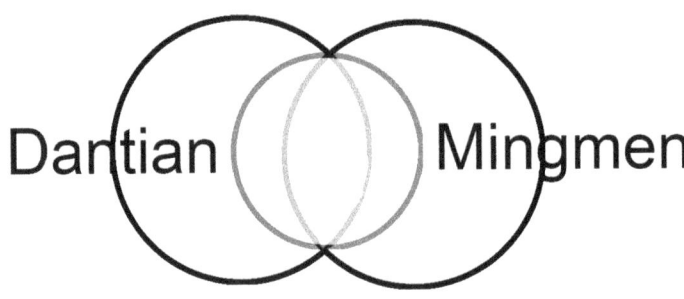

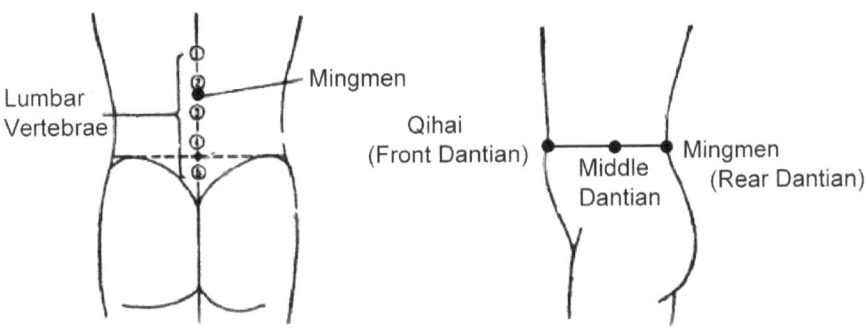

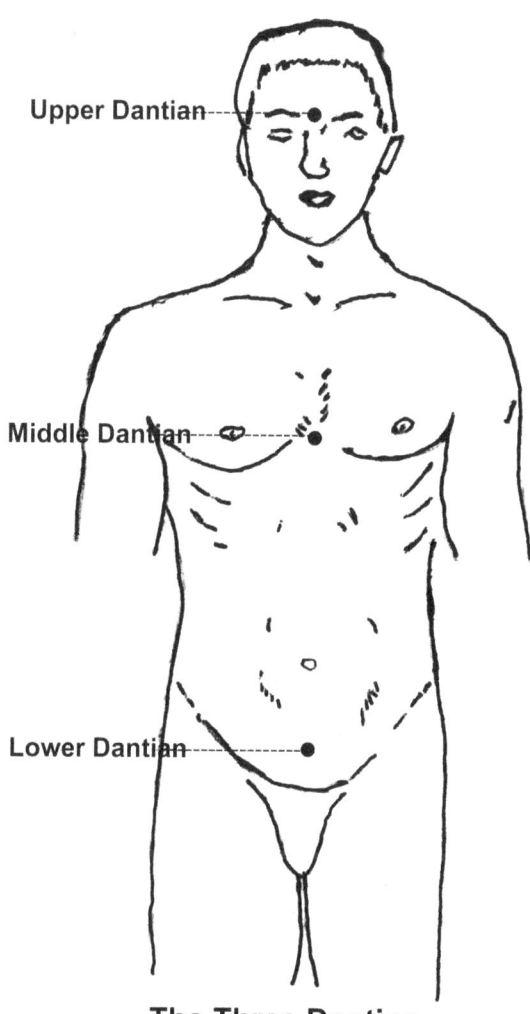

The Three Dantian

Opening the Meridians

One of the purposes of foundational training in Ba Gua Zhang and Nei Gong is to "open the meridians." Opening the meridians means to unblock them so that there is an unobstructed flow of vital energy through these pathways. This also opens the pathways for smooth, unobstructed movement of *Qi* and efficient release of power and strength through the Sinew Channels. Unblocking and opening the meridians in turn opens the body and mind to the universe around us, so that we can sense the health and vitality of our own body in relation to the natural forces that act upon us at every moment. Jonathan Snowiss, a teacher of internal Chinese arts, uses the analogy of a ventilation system. The meridians are like air ducts and the acu-points are like vents on those ducts. If the ducts and vents are closed, the system becomes clogged and the circulation of air is impeded. If they are open, air flows freely and stale air and pathogens can be flushed out and replaced by clean air.[40]

The Du and Ren Channels, which run up and down the centerline of the body, are the "master meridians" in the sense that when they open, the other meridians can also open. These two channels form an integrated circuit that is sometimes referred to as the "Central Channel." It is said that when one meridian opens (the Central Channel), the hundred meridians can open. So by opening the Ren and Du, we facilitate the opening of all the other meridians.

The Importance of Qi

To sum up, *Qi* is something that can be felt, internally sensed and understood, but it cannot be seen, measured or quantified. We sense *Qi* and we can observe its manifestations and effects, but we cannot easily define it, so words often confuse the issue, which is why many teachers in the internal arts do not say much about *Qi*. However, one should keep in mind that this reluctance to talk about *Qi*, rather than negating its importance, actually underscores it.

---

[40] *Wei Tuo Qi Gong – Climbing the Mountain: The Essence of Qi Gong and Martial Arts*, by Jonathan Snowiss. Xlibris, 2010, pp.94-5.

The Purpose of Internal Martial Arts

Teachers of internal martial arts repeatedly say that the internal arts are not just for fighting and that approaching these arts with only this purpose in mind will ultimately lead to disappointment. Internal martial arts have three purposes, which are expressed in the following triad:

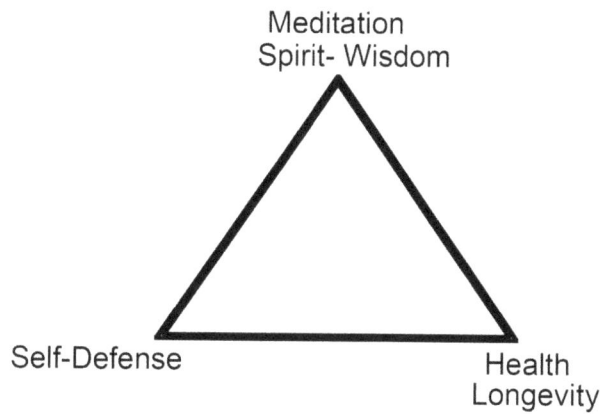

This requires a balanced approach to training:
- Breathing methods
- Health exercises and Nei Gong
- Martial techniques
- Form and technique as an expression of core principles
- Training in harmony with seasons
- Weapons as an extension of hand methods
- Training as meditation – stillness within movement and movement within stillness

Instinct, Self-Knowledge and Wisdom in Internal Martial Arts

Part of the purpose of internal martial arts is to reconnect with the original instinctive energies of the human organism. The relaxed mental focus and internal stillness, combined with correct body alignment, breathing, relaxation, and opening the meridians aims at reconnecting to the "True Breath," the primordial Yin Yang current that flows between Heaven and Earth. This reconnection reinvigorates one's life force, so that *Qi* and breath can enter the bone marrow, tendons, ligaments, flesh and muscle, restoring the pliability of these structures. At they same time we strengthen our connection to our own innate wisdom, thereby re-inciting the life force and its manifestations in the world around us. This "re-incitement" becomes ongoing, allowing creativity and self-knowledge to flourish through an internal resonance between the fundamental universal forces, instinctive knowledge, and primordial instinctive movement that function outside the conscious mind. This ability is a necessary pre-condition for attaining a high level of skill in martial arts. Sensing changes in a situation, or an opponent, before they manifest consciously, is one of the hallmarks of a master practitioner in any field. In the martial arts, great masters use this fine-tuned sensitivity to avoid or deflect conflicts before they can fully develop.

The Nei Gong Triad

In internal martial arts and in internal exercises one needs to engage with the following triad:

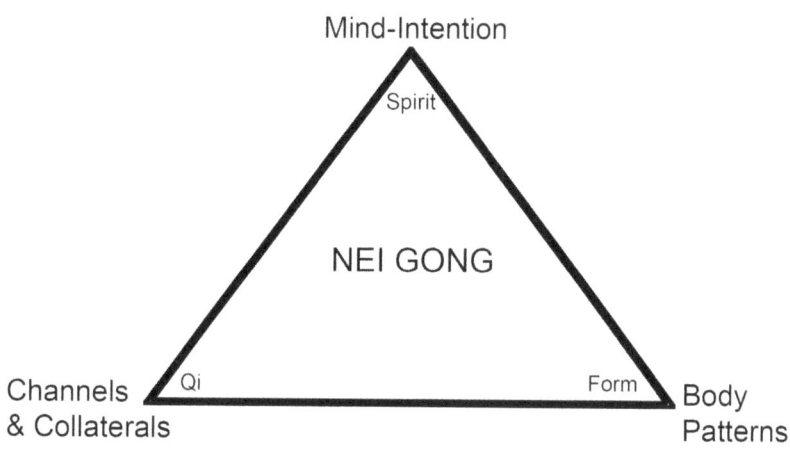

Teachers of *Nei Gong* and the internal martial arts often say that to really understand these practices, and to understand *Qi*, one has to understand Chinese medicine. Further, they emphasize three key points that are critical to learning *Nei Gong* and internal martial arts correctly.

1. It is necessary to have a thorough understanding of the *Jing-Luo* (meridians) in order to practice Nei Gong correctly.

2. It is necessary to have a thorough understanding of the postures and forms, the internal and external body alignments and the methods of moving and changing between the postures and forms.

3. The mind must be tranquil and calm. The Mind-Intention (*Yi*) must permeate all postures and movements.

In training and application, these three elements – the three points of the triangle above – operate as an organic and indivisible whole. Interestingly, these same three points are echoed repeatedly in passages from *Nei Gong Zhen Chuan* (*Authentic Classic of Nei Gong*):

> 1. *Real knowledge of Nei Gong requires a thorough understanding of the vessels and collaterals.*[41]

> 2. *Once the vessels and collaterals are understood you must observe the patterns. After one is familiar with the channels and collaterals it is necessary to understand that there are certain patterns that pertain to the whole body. If the patterns are not understood, all discussion of the channels and collaterals is empty talk.*[42]

> 3. *Once Zhenqi (True Qi) is sufficient in the interior, its external expression will manifest. Although it is hidden inside and unmoving, numinous brilliance is expressed outwardly through the face so that people cannot look at it directly. The Qi stirs from the form, while form follows the Qi. The mind is the master of the spirit and the spirit is the master of the Qi. Therefore, when the Shenqi takes residence, the form will no longer be a burden and one will be like a dragon soaring in the clouds, a bird flying in the emptiness of the sky, coming suddenly and going.*[43]

The base of the Nei Gong Triad consists of the *Jing-Luo* (channels and collaterals, commonly called "the meridians") and the body patterns or forms. The channels and collaterals are the pathways of the *Qi*. They are like rivers, lakes, canals and irrigation ditches that spread *Qi*, blood and fluids throughout the body. The Ren Mai (Conception Vessel) and Du Mai (Governing Vessel), which run up along the midline of the body (in the front and back respectively), are the most

---

[41] *Nei Gong: The Authentic Classic – A Translation of the Nei Gong Zhen Chuan,* translated by Tom Bisio, Huang Guo-Qi and Joshua Paynter. (Denver: Outskirts Press Inc, 2011) p. 3.
[42] Ibid, p. 7.
[43] Ibid, p. 23.

important vessels to cultivate, open and unblock in Daoist inner alchemy practices, internal martial arts and Nei Gong. *Qi* turns and transforms constantly between the Ren and Du vessels. Once these vessels open, it is said that "the hundred meridians will open." Ren and Du are two of the Eight Extraordinary Channels, important meridians that must free flowing in order to carry enough Yang *Qi* to ensure optimal functioning. When the Eight Extraordinary meridians are open and unblocked, one can connect with the primordial consciousness and the authentic self. However, the channels must not be forced open. In Ba Gua Zhang one of the goals is to open the channels up gradually through correct application of form, body patterns and the intention.

Qi does not move easily through tense or blocked areas. Correct posture and alignment, in which the limbs are curved and the joint spaces are open and free, helps the muscles and tissues to relax while simultaneously unblocking circulation. This is akin to water flowing smoothly through a hose that is not kinked or sharply bent. The postures and body patterns (*Shi*) used in internal arts like Ba Gua Zhang, facilitate this relaxed free flow and set up alignments in which the circulation of *Qi* is not only not blocked, but is actually augmented and amplified.

What is meant by body patterns? *Ding Shi* (定式), or "fixed pattern" circle walking, is perhaps **the** key foundational practice in Ba Gua Zhang. *Ding* means "fixed" or "definite," and at the same time it conveys a sense of calm stability. *Shi* means posture or pattern. Similarly in Xing Yi Quan, *San Ti Shi* (the "three body posture") is the key Nei Gong practice, which forms the foundation from which all the other movements and techniques manifest. *San Ti Shi* and *Ding Shi* are patterns of interconnected and interacting body alignments, more akin to the warp and weave of a rug rather than mere external postures. The "pattern" in the context of the practice Xing Yi, Ba Gua and Nei Gong includes an interweaving of the body alignments, the intention, *Qi* and *Jin*.[44]

Qi is the foundation of form (body patterns), but without form *Qi* cannot manifest functionally. Opening of the meridians, in conjunction with the body patterns, calms and stabilizes the Spirit, thereby transforming consciousness, but at the same time opening the meridians is itself dependent on the Heart-Mind and Spirit being calm and stable. Therefore, each element of this triad simultaneously acts on and is acted upon, by the other two elements. In this way, internal training is an organic inter-connected, living whole. Understanding and progress in one area of training necessarily facilitates understanding and progress in every other area.

---

[44] 劲 *Jin*: a vigorous and lively expression of refined power and strength.

BA GUA ZHANG AS EXERCISE & PHYSICAL THERAPY

8

Some Ba Gua masters consider Ba Gua to be the ultimate Nei Gong exercise because it is the culmination of a tradition of *Dao Yin* (guiding, pulling and leading *Qi* exercises), *Tu Na* (breathing exercises), Nei Gong (internal exercises), martial arts, Daoist meditation, Daoist alchemical practices, and other *Yang Sheng* (Life Nourishing) practices that date back at least as far as the early Han dynasty. Because of the relatively late development of Ba Gua Zhang as a martial art (the founder, Dong Hai Chuan, lived from 1813 to 1882), Ba Gua draws on all of these traditions and, according to some experts, incorporated the best methods from these various traditions into its techniques and training methods.

Ba Gua as an exercise method is second to none. Its basic practices work with breath, alignment, balance, coordination and the development of unified body power. The varied standing and circle walking postures strengthen the joints and open the meridians, while twisting the fascia. In the intermediate and advanced training the body is in constant motion, twisting, turning, spiraling. Partner exercises act as a kind of resistance training combined with inner listening and sensing. Weapon training also acts a form of resistance training, but in addition refines motor skills and spatial awareness. The mind and spirit are fully engaged when practicing Ba Gua. This engagement develops a relaxed, focused awareness similar to methods of mediation.

In contrast to many modern approaches to exercise, Ba Gua is integral and organic. I constantly read or hear of people who cobble together training methods, which attempt to combine yoga, weight training, cardiovascular exercise and proprioceptive exercises, as well as skill and agility training in a disconnected fashion. This kind of disconnection often confuses the body and sets it up for injury. This is similar to studying several martial arts with conflicting training methods simultaneously. One's progress is impaired, because the mind and body are receiving mixed messages. In my Chinese medicine clinic in New York City, I specialized in sports and orthopedic injuries. A fairly large percentage of people hurt themselves, not from playing sports, but by doing exercises that were supposed to maintain health or actually *prevent* injury.

This is also true in the realm of physical therapy and specialized sports training regimens. There are countless methods that promise to teach you to move naturally, or to move like an animal, a leopard or a tiger. Close examination shows that these methods are extracting basic mechanical principles about the relationship of power and flexibility to posture and body alignment that have been understood in China for centuries, if not a millennium. There is nothing wrong with this approach, except that usually individual aspects of these principles tend to be dissected and presented out of context, rather than linked as an organic whole. This makes them hard to learn and implement on an unconscious level. The ancient Chinese made very detailed observations about animals and what humans could learn from their instinctive movements and inner nature. They recorded the specific qualities that could be developed by adopting the natural movements of animals. Over thousand of years Chinese sages, martial artists and physicians created exercises and forms to develop these qualities. This has nothing to do with a Jackie Chan movie where he performs the snake or crane style. Ba Gua practitioners look at the natural internal movement of an animal, and how it dynamically manifests, power, flexibility and coordinated movement, rather than simply imitating the external movement and look of the animal.

If you are practicing Ba Gua Zhang mainly for exercise and health, you do not need to learn all facets of the art, but the more facets of the art you do embrace, the more balanced and complete your fitness and health will be. The beauty of this kind of complete practice is that each part of Ba Gua Zhang integrates and compliments every other part. So you don't have to learn 10 different things, but instead are delving more and more deeply into one thing - an organically complete art form. Many students learn only the foundational level of the art, and yet experience vast changes in many aspects of fitness and health. This is because the foundation contains the seeds of the advanced training. Advanced training is not only contingent on first building a solid foundation, but is also hidden within the foundation and can be discovered by a diligent student even without the teacher's help. In this sense, Ba Gua Zhang has a fractal-like structure.

Ba Gua Zhang has many movements that "open" and mobilize the joints. These movements creates more space within the joint capsule, which in turn allows fluids to more freely into the joint space and nourish the articular surfaces of the joint. When a joint space is in this open position, it can more freely rotate through its range of motion in a manner that properly connects it to other joints in the kinematic chain. This also strengthens the small intrinsic muscles that support and protect the joint.

In recent years cutting edge physical therapy has discovered that just improving circulation through cardio-vascular activity and strengthening muscles through resistance training often does not yield the desired results, particularly when it comes to sports injuries. There is a growing realization that people often lose proprioception in the injured area. Proprioception is the sense of the relative position of neighboring parts of the body and strength of effort being employed in movement. In humans, proprioception is provided by receptors in skeletal muscles, tendons and the fibrous joint capsules. The brain and nervous system integrate information from these receptors and from the vestibular system, to create an overall sense of body position, movement, and acceleration. Therefore, exercises that increase and target proprioception are often more important than strengthening muscles. For example, with repeated ankle injuries, ligaments in the ankle can become lax and overstretched. Physical therapists discovered that isolated muscle strengthening exercise did little for this problem, because the problem was not so much weakness, but a lack of connection to the rest of the leg and the core of the body. Hence the current focus on exercises like standing on one leg and reaching in different directions with the other leg (sounds a bit like mud-stepping), or standing on a wobble board, both of which challenge one's balance and perception of the body in space.

Tensegrity ("tension-integrity") is a term originally coined by Buckminster Fuller. It is often used to describe the elastic nature of the facial web and its connection to the bones. In the model pictured below, the rods are like the bones and the elastic strings like the fascia. When the model is compressed or put under tension, the compressive force is distributed equally throughout the structure. When compression is released, it springs back to its original position.

The tensegrity of the fascia is reproduced down to the cellular level. This allows the body's structure to distribute stress throughout the entire system, thereby remaining resilient to the effects of external forces. The curved, bow-like spiraling of the spine and limbs used in postures and movements of internal martial arts maximizes this aspect of the body's ability to retain its shape and structure under elastic compression.

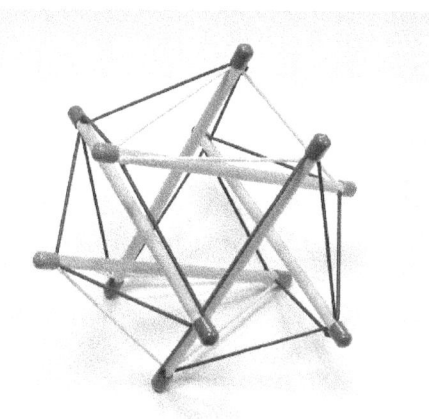

Tensegrity Model

Thomas Myers, author of the best-selling book *Anatomy Trains: Myofascial Meridians for Manual and Movement Therapists,* feels that the focus on muscles in most exercise systems is misguided and advocates activities, which maintain the pliability of the fascia. He gives the following advice:

- Do whole body stretching that stretches the fascial planes in multiple directions (like movements found in Tai Ji, Ba Gua and Yoga).

- Both walking and running help maintain whole body elasticity.

- Go slowly so that the fascia can stretch easily and smoothly.

- The best way to train the facial net is to engage in whole body movements that constantly challenge the body.

- Avoid machines and repetitive movements that work in the same line repeatedly.

- Avoid isolated muscle movement.[45]

All of these components are a part of Ba Gua Zhang Training and may relate to what internal martial artists call "sinew strength" or "tendon strength," to differentiate the elastic power of connected fascial chains from muscular strength. In fact, Myers' "Myofascial Meridians" were already known more than 1,000 years ago as the Sinew Channels or Tendino-Muscular Meridians.

From a clinical perspective, arts like Ba Gua Zhang, Tai Ji Quan, and Xing Yi Quan are effective as physical therapy because they look at the body as an interconnected whole. In my clinic I frequently saw people who were misdiagnosed and treated ineffectively because of the tendency to try and reduce dysfunction to one factor that can be understood by modern imaging equipment, so that obvious alternative possibilities were overlooked. For example, numbness in the hands is a problem often attributed to a disc problem in the neck. Because many people over the age of 30 have a bulging disc in the neck that shows up on an MRI or X-ray, the assumption is that the disc is the problem, when far more often it is muscular and fascial imbalances causing neck and shoulder tightness that impinge on the thoracic inlet. Acupuncture and bodywork often provide temporary relief, but Nei Gong exercises re-educate the body and the fascia, solving the problem and preventing relapse.

The internal organs are also connected by the fascial network and can be affected by tissue tension imbalances in the Sinew Channels and the fascia that wraps the organs. Organ dysfunctions often start from chronic imbalances in the elasticity and resilience of these envelopes of connective tissue. Osteopaths who correct these tensions using manual

---

[45] Staying Fit All Life Long: 10 Tips for Fascial Fitness Tom Myers www.embody-work.com/.../Tom-Myers-10-Tips-for-Fascial-Fitness.pdf and *Fascial Fitness: Training in the Neuro-Fascial Web,* by Thomas Myers April 2011 IDEA Fitness Journal

fascial release techniques have found that improvements in organ function are a by-product of this corrective manipulation. Likewise, acupuncture at distal points on the limbs aids organ function through the Sinew Channels and the deeper channels, which run through the peritoneal tissue. Nei Gong exercises affect the organs through these same mechanisms, by pulling on and realigning the tissue that wraps the organs through the fascial chains that make up the Sinew Channels.

The oldest medical manuscripts in China were found in Changsha, in the Mawangdui tombs from the early Han dynasty (2nd century BCE). Some of these manuscripts contain longevity techniques and exercises that were used as a means of preventing disease and attaining long life. Many of these exercises depict various kinds of medical exercise, including stretching movements that relieve or "pull" pain from various areas in the body. Some movements depict ways of modifying or balancing Yin and Yang, while others are described as: *enhancing Qi flow in the eight extraordinary channels.*[46]

Donald Harper suggests that these early medical manuscripts combined ideas about muscles and blood vessels leading to what today we call channels and collaterals or meridians.[47] In practice, the channels and collaterals (meridians) interpenetrate with the muscles, fascia, tendons, bone, and the internal organs in an interconnected network. The ancient *Dao Yin* exercises apparently used massage-like movements and stretches to lead, guide and tug the *Qi* in specific ways. Today, Nei Gong

---

[46] *Chinese Healing Exercises* by Livia Kohn (Honolulu: University of Hawai'i Press, 2008) p.43.
[47] *Early Chinese Medical Literature: The Mawangdui Manuscripts,* Translation and Study by Donald Harper (London and New York: Kegan Paul International, 1998) p. 83.

practitioners use breath, posture, movement, and intention to contract and relax, align, and re-orient the fascia, muscles, and tendons, ligaments, and bones in order to stretch, and to open and close the meridians as well as expand and contract the cavities that contain the internal organs. Employing movement in coordination with carefully directed Mind-Intention can modify the functional activities that Chinese medicine attributes to the internal organs. An important part of the tradition of Qi Gong and Nei Gong can be understood to operate to some degree by modification of the flow of *Qi* and fluids through the fascia and the *Jing Luo* (Meridian) system.

The Yin Yang Fish Palm
Opens & Stimulates the Belt Channel (Dai Mai)

Ba Gua Zhang & Nei Gong

There are many forms of Nei Gong that are related to the internal martial arts.

Over the centuries these Nei Gong exercises have been used both as a kind of advanced athletic training to enhance physical performance, hence their inclusion in the martial arts. They have also been employed as a kind of physical therapy to rebalance and rehabilitate the body. Some of these methods are also part of Daoist self-cultivation practices. A few key examples of very powerful and effective Nei Gong sets are:

- Muscle Tendon Change (*Yi Jin Jing*): strengthens the sinews and the entire body.

- Silk Reeling Exercises (*Duan Jin*): develops winding, spiral, whole-body power.

- Marrow Washing Nei Gong (*Xi Sui Jing*): strengthens the bones, brain, and nervous system.

- Five Animal Play (*Wu Chin Xi*): harmonizes the five organs and strengthens the body, while developing coordination and agility by imitating the movements of animals.

- Micro-Cosmic Orbit Meditation or Small Heavenly Circle *(Xiao Zhou Tian Gong)*: opens up the Central Channel and by extension the entire meridian system.

- Macro-Cosmic Orbit Meditation or Great Heavenly Circle (*Da Zhou Tian Gong*): opens up all the meridians and regulates Yin and Yang.

- Standing Meditation or Stake Standing (*Zhan Zhuang*): develops rooted, whole body strength.

Ba Gua Zhang has adopted some of these practices into its training methods and some of these exercises serve as adjunctive training regimens for students. However, the genius of Ba Gua Zhang is that is it was able to benefit from many of these older methods and absorb their key elements into the Circle Walking Nei Gong practice. The Circle Walking practice integrates the principles and internal aspects of all of these powerful Nei Gong methods into a single exercise, so that they can be developed simultaneously, rather than by sequentially practicing each of the Nei Gong method independently. This integration is not only more efficient, but also inherently more unified and natural.

BA GUA ZHANG AS A MARTIAL ART

People often wonder how slow movements, performed lightly and smoothly without a partner, teach effective self-defense skills. Slow movement allows you to relax and sense inside. One of the things you are sensing are the places where you are tense, and how this tension inhibits your natural reflexes and your ability to generate power and speed. Relaxation increases speed and power. Practicing forms and movements in a relaxed, smooth fashion also calms the mind and relaxes the nervous system, so that it can properly modulate the body's actions and slowly begin to unlearn the habits of body and mind that restrict free movement and the body's natural expression of power, grace and speed.

Training slowly and smoothly improves coordination and balance. Balance is critical to martial arts. At the foundational level, the internal martial arts stress balance and "rootedness," the ability to maintain balance and stay centered against outside forces such as a powerful push. Many students notice after a year or two of training Standing Meditation and Circle Walking Nei Gong that in sparring practice, or during a collision on a crowded street, the other person seems to bounce off of them.

The smooth relaxed forms and movements of Ba Gua Zhang teach the body to move as an integrated whole, so that when one part moves every part moves. Integrated whole body movement is very difficult to learn when one practices movements too fast. Integration must be acquired through patient, slow movement. Only then can it be applied at high speed. Practicing in a continuous, smooth, unbroken fashion allows one's instinctive movement to naturally unfold. The result is continuous action and movement, without the need to pause and reset. In this way, defense and offense blend into a unified, dynamic flow of movement.

In Ba Gua Zhang, the alignment of the body and the slow, even movement of the steps allows the body to conserve *Qi,* so that *Qi* begins to gather in *Dantian.* Consolidating *Qi* in *Dantian* in turn allows *Qi* to gather and release simultaneously, recharging the body with every step.

Master Zhao Da Yuan Demonstrates the Piercing Palm

The movements contained within the Ba Gua forms are deceptive, partly because they are simultaneously both abstract and specific. On one hand, the movements are about movement patterns rather than specific techniques. These patterns contain unlimited potential for change and transformation. This limitless potential is expressed in the idea that a single movement can manifest in 10,000 techniques. The same movement can be a throw, a strike, an off-balancing maneuver, joint lock etc. On the other hand, each form also expresses a particular geometry – a kind of "motion, time, distance equation" that reveals specific techniques and attacks to specific vital points, which can then transform in synchrony with changes in distance and position.

Simply inculcating these movement patterns in the body can produce effective self-defense. I have had several students, who only had rudimentary training in the basic exercises and Circle Walking Nei Gong, successfully navigate "street" situations through the instinctual response created by their practice. In one case, a mentally disturbed patient in the hospital attacked the student, a physician who studied Ba Gua. He merely turned into a single palm change and the attacker went flying by him into the wall. The patient came at him again and the same thing happened. At that point, others stepped in to subdue the attacker. A similar thing happened to a student who was about to exit an elevator, when a man trying to trap her in the elevator accosted her. She turned, in her words "just like in class," and he fell into the elevator while she stepped out.

Of course for Ba Gua to be a truly effective martial art, one must also practice with a partner and learn specific martial techniques that are expressions of the forms. This means learning parries, strikes, throws, how to lock and control joints, conditioning parts of the body for impact, etc. Specific martial techniques are important parts of any martial art, and in an art like Ba Gua, which seamlessly blends kicking, punching locking and throwing with evasive footwork, there are many specific skills to learn.

However without the *Gong Fu*, the internalization of foundational skills and attributes, all one has is a body of techniques that will be difficult to apply against an opponent who does not cooperate. This is why Chinese masters place so much emphasis on the basics. In the words of Li Zi Ming:

I have a school brother. He is honest and did not speak much. He did not learn very many boxing sets and methods, but he walked the circle his whole life. As a result, his skill was excellent and other martial arts practitioners could not get close to his body when fighting with him. The reason is that his thought was pure and he mastered the skill of circle walking and obtained powerful strength. What strength is it? I think it is mainly the arousal of Qi that can strengthen and safeguard the body through the unity of Qi and power. This kind of unity cannot be defeated simply by seizing and grasping skills.[48]

Health and Self Defense

Ba Gua Zhang, like all the internal boxing arts, is for both health and self-defense. On a very basic level, this duality is evident in the breathing and body alignment practices that form the foundation of the internal martial arts. These fundamental practices are said to aid health by improving basic body functions and increased resistance to disease. The same foundational exercises are also used to develop increased efficiency in the underlying mechanics of self-defense movements. The importance of both aspects of the internal martial arts cannot be emphasized enough. Practitioners who focus on one aspect to the expense of the other often fail to achieve their goals, and are disappointed with the results of their training.

The Benefits of Partner Work

Some students are nervous about the self-defense aspect of Ba Gua Zhang. Yet practicing self-defense skills, and maintaining efficiency and calm in the face of an attack, prepares us for other outside forces that can so easily affect us, whether they be irritating noises, a stressful work place,

---

[48] *A Brief Introduction to the Body Strengthening Function of the Eight Diagram Palm Qi Gong* by Li Zi Ming, Translated by Huang Guo Qi, (Pa Kua Chang Journal Vol. 5 No. 1 Nov./Dec. 1994, Pacific Grove CA: High View Publications) p. 17-19.

or an abusive boss. In a sense, practicing with a partner is like resistance training to develop strength. Whether you are practicing rolling hands sensitivity exercises, individual techniques or free styling with techniques (technique sparring), your partner's force challenges your ability to maintain structure. His or her force loads more force into your body. This creates a direct increase in strength over time. Another principle that one learns through partner practice is to deflect and redirect our partner's force, attempting to let him or her fall into emptiness.

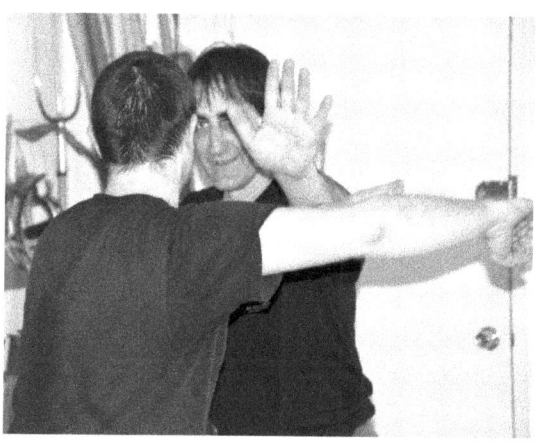

These skills have many implications for human interaction beyond hand-to-hand combat and physical self-defense. Partner practice does not just make the body stronger, it also forges a strong mind and spirit. Through correct self-defense training, the innate resilience of the human organism can be exponentially increased, conveying enormous health benefits that are rarely produced by meditation and health exercises alone.

**Gao Ji Wu Demonstrates an Application of
Golden Threads Brushing the Eyebrows**

Gao Ji Wu talked to me about how his Nei Gong practice and understanding of the meaning of the movements vis-a-vis combat helps him weather the vicissitudes of life. In moments of difficulty and anger, he falls back on his training, which helps him proceed with calm equanimity. Master Gao also says that it is important to understand the meaning of a technique. For example, that in a particular movement we are striking a vital point or even attacking the eyes. He then quickly and emphatically added, "but in your whole life you would never do those things!" Understanding the meaning of the movements trains the mind and spirit, which are important aspects of preserving both one's health and the integrity of the art. Master Zhao Da Yuan, who emphasizes effective combat techniques in his teaching, almost exactly echoed this sentiment. Master Zhao says that realistic training hones the body, mind and spirit, but the techniques should not be used to harm others, unless you are fighting for your life or the lives of innocent people.

Likewise, it is also important to embrace the health promoting aspects of training in the internal martial arts. Practicing only the self-defense aspects of the internal arts can damage one's health, ultimately weakening the ability to defend oneself. Ironically, this is a self-defeating equation. The hard training that many martial artists endure in order to perfect combat skills can take a serious toll on one's health and vitality, if not balanced properly with common sense and methods that protect and nurture the health of the body. In the end, protecting your health and ability to function well into old age is the ultimate self-defense

Circle Walking as the Basis of Martial Skill

The acme of Ba Gua Zhang as a martial art is to walk so as to stand next to the opponent, or even to move behind him, while he falls into the void – the space you just vacated. This does not mean running around someone to get behind them, but rather to use the inherent force and misdirection contained in circular movement to one's advantage. It is this concept in particular that invites comparisons between Ba Gua Zhang and guerilla warfare. A circle, unlike a line, has no discernable beginning and end points. When using circular steps, one is simultaneously going forward and backward, and advancing and retreating, while the body rotates. The step automatically creates the tactical changes, because the nature of an arced, circular step, combined with body rotation is such that, although you are constantly moving forward toward the opponent, it seems to the opponent as though you are retreating and vacating the space he or she is trying to enter.

Circular stepping has the effect of "dropping the opponent into emptiness" and allows you to move to his rear in a single flowing step, rather than the two-beat action of a sidestep and counter-attack. The result is that you seem to "disappear." Moving in this fashion is sometimes described as "escaping and melting away" or "escaping and changing the shadow." The emphasis on escape and evasion in Ba Gua means that the goal in a physical encounter is not so much to "win" as to "prevail" – which might mean downing the opponent, but might just as equally mean to escape or avoid the encounter without bodily harm.

Sun Zhi Jun Walking with the Millstone Pushing Palm

Ba Gua's smooth steps are variable. Cheng Style Master Sun Zhi Jun is renowned for his ability to take extremely long steps while maintaining power and correct body alignment. The smoothness of Gao Ji Wu's steps make you think he is still in front of you when he has already turned your corner.

Zhang Hua Sen surprised me more than once with the speed of his short, quick steps, which could cover a surprising amount of ground while simultaneously making subtle adjustments in angle and direction.

Zhang Hua Sen was responsible for one of my first revelations about stepping and the importance of the correct positioning of the feet in Ba Gua Zhang. He was teaching applications to myself and another student applications. My partner was quite strong and we were working on an uprooting push using the Mountain Pushing Palm. My push had little effect. Zhang walked over and slightly adjusted the position of my *Koubu* (hook step), which was behind my partner's foot. I pushed again, no harder than before, but this time he flew up in the air and landed flat on his back. We were both surprised!

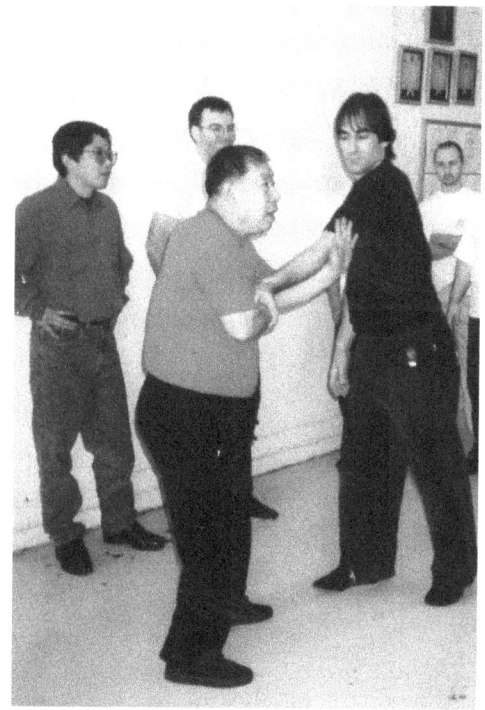

Zhang Hu Sen teaching in NYC (1998)

Ba Gua's unorthodox approach to fighting, which avoids confrontation and favors escape and evasion, has similarities to guerilla warfare. Guerilla warfare subverts the normal clashing of fighters and/or armies, which often heavily relies on power, numbers and strength of the defensive posture. It subverts this direct approach by being dynamic, continuously changing, transforming and moving. Guerilla warfare does not rely on static defense or direct attack. In guerrilla actions one seeks to avoid battle, evading direct engagements in which damage and attrition might be suffered. In Ba Gua, avoiding direct engagement is achieved through hit-and-run tactics, which employ timing, footwork, turning, and evasion combined with the use of "hidden kicks and ambushing hands." Mao Ze Dong described guerrilla warfare as "constant activity and movement" and Che Guevara described it as a dance or a minuet. When the engagement starts, and the enemy advances, the guerrilla band retreats, maintaining contact while an attack is initiated from another point. Ba Gua has also been likened to a dance in which one moves next to and revolves around one's opponent, leading him to the left and right, front and back, up and down.

Guerilla warfare is often described as unorthodox warfare. In the same way Ba Gua deliberately chooses to employ unorthodox methods. In the "Eight Contraries," differences between fighting strategies in Ba Gua and those in other styles of fighting are delineated: *Everyone advances forward with a straight step, but we advance on an angle with a twisted step, Everyone likes to show various gestures, but we just wait to move in the stillness. Everyone likes to turn the whole body around to face the rear, but in a single step we can move to deal with the eight directions.*[49]

---

[49] *Liang Zhen Pu Eight Diagram Palm*, Li Zi Ming, compiled and edited by Vincent Black (High View Publications: Pacific Grove, CA, 1993) p. 18.

Stages of Ba Gua Zhang Training

Ba Gua training proceeds in stages, beginning with developmental training which builds the foundation for more advanced training.

1. Basic Post Standing Exercises (*Zhan Zhuang*): Standing while holding a fixed posture is a pre-requisite for training forms and martial skills. Standing allows you to perceive and connect with the subtle, natural and spontaneous movements occurring inside the body.

2. The 28 Foundational Exercises: The Foundational Exercises build physical coordination, strength and relaxed power, while loosening and opening up all the joints of the body. The 28 Exercises also develop the building- block movements upon which more advanced movements are based.

HawkPosture

3. Twelve Standing Postures: These twelve postures develop power and root in different stances and the ability to shift smoothly from one stance to another. Holding the postures strengthens the sinews and bones, creates fascial twists that run through the body that magnify power, and opens specific meridians and organ cavities so that *Qi* can flow smoothly. Practicing the twelve postures in a fluid, connected chain also develops specific fighting applications and agile foot, hand and body work

4. Circle Walking Nei Gong (Ding Shi Ba Gua Zhang): This is **the** key exercise in learning and mastering Ba Gua Zhang. Circle Walking Nei Gong strengthens the body, gathers *Qi* in *Dantian*, develops unified whole-body power and agility, trains footwork and defensive and attacking skills, and opens and unblocks the meridians. The postures and the transitions between the postures are easily translated into throwing, striking and off-balancing techniques.

5. Foundational Partner Exercises: The Foundational Partner Exercises teach the basic movements of blocking and striking, develop power, and teach basic martial skills.

6. Old Eight Palms (*Lao Ba Zhang*): The Eight Palm Changes are the basis of all the other changes, forms and techniques. Each palm teaches different body actions, footwork, strategies and techniques.

7. Eight Hands: (*Ba Shou*): Linear expressions of the Eight Palm Changes that have direct and obvious applications to self-defense.

8. Tian Gan (Heavenly Stem) Exercises: Tian Gan wrings out the spine, thereby freeing restrictions that inhibit power and mobility. At the same time, these exercises isolate and develop many of the power dynamics found in *Lao Ba Zhang*.

**A Young Wang Shi Tong
Demonstrating the Uplifting Palm**

9. *Rou Shou* **(Yielding Hands):** Also called *Fan Gun Shou* (Overturning & Rolling Hands). These two-person exercises develop the ability to stick to your partner/opponent and lead him or her while walking and changing direction. There are both static and moving *Rou Shou* exercises.

10. Marrow Washing Nei Gong: An advanced Nei Gong practice that strengthens the sinews and bones, brain and spinal cord, and promotes marrow and blood production. Marrow Washing Nei Gong also develops higher-level skills such as power sensing and the simultaneous storage and release of power.

11. Martial Skills Training: throwing (*Shuai Fa*), kicking (*Ti Fa*), striking (*Da Fa*), elbowing (*Zhou Fa*), and seizing and capture skills (*Qin Na*).

119

12. Ba Gua Chain Linking Form (*Ba Gua Lian Huan*): *Lian Huan* is a form that links movements together so that they are smooth and unbroken.

**Master Wang Shi Tong Applies
"Step Forward with the Cutting Elbow" from the 64 Hands**

14. The Sixty-Four Hands (*Liu Shi Si Shou*): The Sixty-Four Hands consist of eight lines of eight movements. Each of these movements illustrates applications of the Eight Palm Changes (*Lao Ba Zhang*), and develops direct attacks characterized by a driving, penetrating power.

15. Technique Sparring: Partner practice in which techniques are combined with rolling hands sensitivity and listening skills. Partners attempt to counter and re-counter each other, while combining different techniques and methods.

Master Gao Ji Wu Demonstrates White Ape Offering Fruit From the 64 Hands

16. Eight Animal Pre-Heaven Form (*Xian Tian Xiang Xing Zhang*): The Eight Animals of Ba Gua and their tactics and movements. This form develops the ability to change the external form and internal power dynamic through changing the intention.

17. Sparring: Freestyle practice of Ba Gua Zhang against unrehearsed attacks.

18. Advanced Forms and Techniques: The Changing Palms, Cloud Swimming Dragon Palm and Eight Direction Palms. These advanced forms teach many techniques while refining one's footwork, fluidity and body mechanics.

19. Weapons Training: Saber, Sword, Staff, Spear, Seven Star Walking Stick, Ba Gua Cane, Rooster Claw Knives, Hook Sickle Swords, Mandarin Duck Knives, Wind Wheel Swords, Elbow Knives, Point Striking Stick.

20. Seated Meditation Practice: Different forms of seated meditation derived from Daoist and Buddhist traditions. Seated meditation provides an excellent counterpoint and balance to Ba Gua's circling, spiraling and changing movements.

The order of training outlined above is idealized. In practice the teacher often adjusts the curriculum according to the needs and abilities of the individual student. Although the basics and foundational skills are generally learned first, there are potentially multiple starting points and paths of study. Learning Ba Gua Zhang is not linear, but circular. Within the training method there is built-in and ongoing recursive learning. Students return to the Foundational Exercises again and again, revisiting the same material, but each time experiencing it from a new vantage point. The fractal-like nature of Ba Gua Zhang means that that core practices like Circle Walking Nei Gong and the Single Palm Change contain all the key principles and methods of movement contained in the entire Ba Gua Zhang system. The learning process consists of repeatedly expanding outward from these seminal core techniques, and then contracting back to the core techniques. This circular, expanding and contracting learning dynamic is diagramed below.

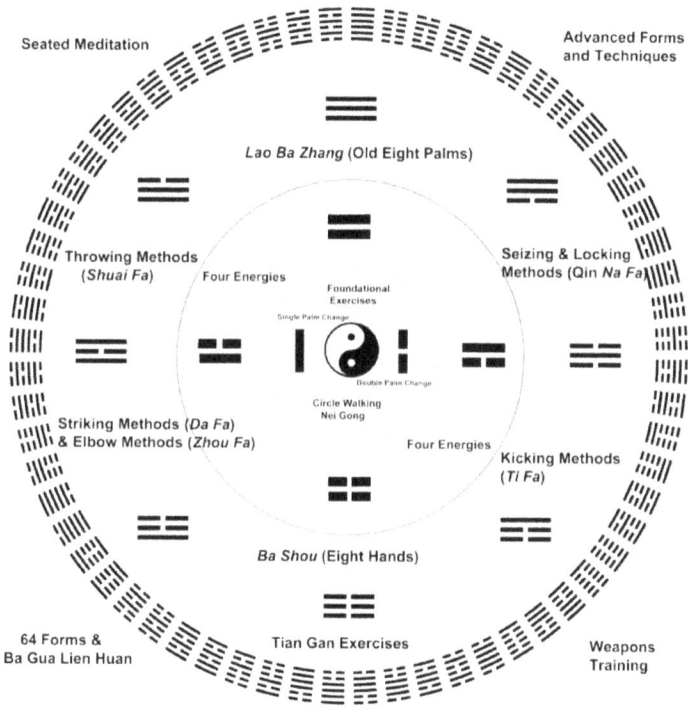

The phases of Ba Gua Zhang Training can also be imaged as a rotating wheel. Each stage interconnects and interpenetrates with each of the other stages via the spokes and hub of the wheel:

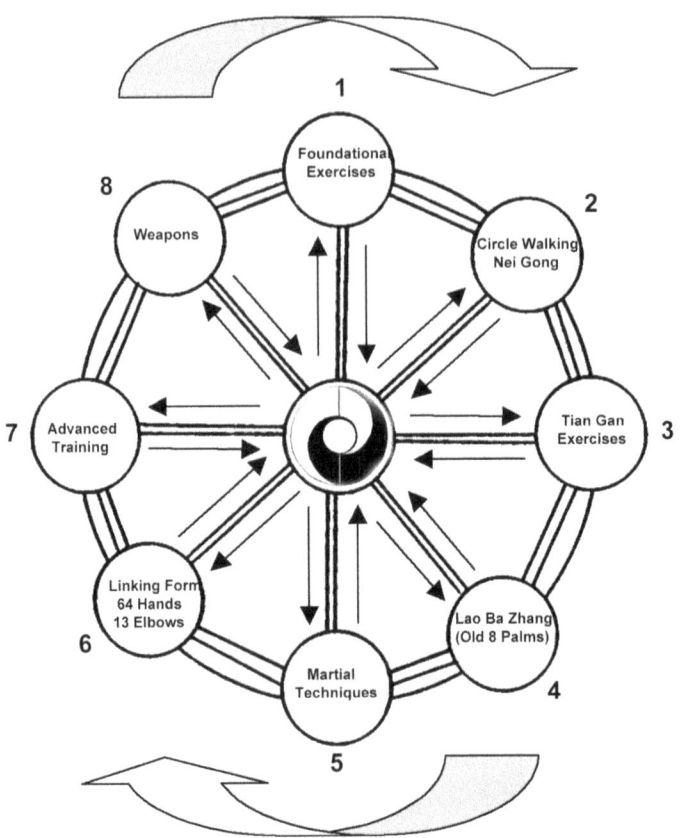

Ba Gua Zhang's Eight Animals

Some styles of Ba Gua use eight animals as images that allow the practitioner to engage with eight different shapes (appearances), eight body patterns, eight kinds of movement and eight kinds of feeling and spirit. In some styles of Ba Gua the "animal form" is simply another way to look at the Circle Walking Nei Gong postures (*Ding Shi Ba Gua Zhang*). In other styles there are specific forms and movements for each animal. The purpose of animal forms is to understand

124

how transforming the *Yi* (intention) changes the mental attitude, spirit, emotion, power generation, strategy and the shape or external form of the body. This understanding allows you to manifest seamless changes and transformations in harmony with changing circumstances. The Eight Animals serve as symbols that represent their different qualities.

The benefit of using symbols like the Eight Animals is that symbols are rich in imagery and serve as an alternative language that by–passes the everyday mind. Symbols allow one to engage with another, more subtle, mode of perception that is not dependent on words and is more conducive to perceiving minute internal energetic changes inside the body. Symbols communicate and crystallize an aspect of direct experience or truth that is beyond words and beyond the symbol itself. In this context, symbols also provide a platform for self-discovery, experimentation and transcendence.

Not all styles of Ba Gua Zhang are in complete agreement about which specific animals constitute the Eight Animals. For example, what some people call the Bear posture (or shape), others call the Tiger. In some styles the Bear is replaced by the Horse. This may seem silly, but not if we keep in mind that:

1. Symbols are a way of encoding a reality and are not the reality itself. Therefore different symbols can be used to understand the same reality.

2. Different teachers perceive different things in Ba Gua's constantly transforming movements and make different associations with different animals.

3. Many individual movements in Ba Gua contain an animal image, for example: "Hawk Spirals Up to Heaven" or "Black Bear Turns it Body." This also leads to different interpretations of the movements.

4. Ba Gua Zhang is not any one animal, but can be viewed as an organic whole that is an integrated composite of the Eight Animals.

The famous Ba Gua teacher Jiang Rong Jiao described Ba Gua by using a series of composite images composed of the Dragon, Monkey, Tiger and Hawk. The continuously flowing circular steps are performed with the "form of a swimming dragon": effortless and natural in appearance, yet within steady and stable. The spirit must be nimble and alert, like a monkey guarding its food, and must be expressed by the attentiveness of the eyes. The leg methods and must have the appearance of a "crouching tiger," calm and powerful. In turning the body, one must be agile and unrestrained, like a hawk spiraling, wheeling, plummeting and turning over in the sky. These are four of the Eight Animals in most styles. In Liang Style Ba Gua Zhang the Eight Animals are:

Snake

The snake is maneuverable and flexible, its *Qi* smooth and unobstructed and its spirit bright and penetrating. The Snake deals effortlessly with obstructions to its movement and changes, never confronting them directly, but either winding around them or penetrating through hidden openings. Like water, the Snake is adaptable and follows the contours of the terrain and the situation, always finding a path for movement and transformation. In combat, the attitude of the Snake is to be like water, impersonally and inexorably adapting to the situation in order to penetrate the opponent's defenses.

Dragon

The Dragon represents potentiated power that is in a state of constant transformation. Although the Dragon is flexible and supple and adaptable like the snake, its adaptability is based on transformation. The Dragon has the ability to be high or low, simultaneously coil and uncoil, and to gather and release energy and power continuously. This ability allows for a continuous generation and renewal. In combat, the Dragon's indomitable attitude stems not from ferocity, but from its unstoppable and continuous transformation that vibrates and pulses back and forth between Yin and Yang, attack and defense, softness and firmness.

Tiger

The Tiger is fierce and indomitable. However, its fierce nature is underscored by intelligence and patience. The Tiger's power relies on its hidden movements in crouching and turning so that its intention and strength gather undetected. Strength and ferocity cannot be seen and then suddenly manifest coming out of nowhere, like a Tiger leaping out of tall grass. When the Tiger moves, it radiates spirit and focused intention. In combat, the Tiger uses the power of the back and legs. The Tiger gathers its power and hides its intention while it waits for an opportunity to spring forward with unstoppable force.

Swallow

The Swallow exudes excitability and is full of energy and spirit. Hence it has been called "the most flexible of birds." This flexibility allows the swallow to be adaptable, using its maneuverability to smoothly get around, under and over obstacles. If cornered, the Swallow can be aggressive and will use every tool at its disposal to prevail over the situation or an opponent. In combat, the Swallow uses its great maneuverability to dodge and counter-attack high and low, and from the left and right, using all its weapons, wings, beak and claws, to overwhelm the opponent though unceasing, swift and continuous movement.

Monkey Form
Master Gao Ji Wu

Monkey

The Monkey is clever and alert, inquisitive and aware, yet within its mind and Heart-Spirit remains tranquil and calm. The Monkey uses its alertness to search for hidden advantages and likes to employ the element of surprise. The Monkey's calm interior allows it to feign madness and capriciousness while remaining cool and collected. When encountering resistance or difficulties, the Monkey employs agility and mobility, in coordination with its intelligence to turn the situation around and prevail. In combat, the Monkey cleverly leads the opponent into over-extending or even underestimating the monkey's strength. Once the opponent is vulnerable the Monkey counterattacks mercilessly.

Horse

The Horse is persistent, valiant and aggressive, charging forward to burst though obstacles. The Horse is also intelligent. It does not charge blindly but twists, dodges and turns, sometimes retreating only to advance again. The Horse's energetic nature drives its boundless potential for advancement and change. In combat, the Horse waits for the opportunity to move in and collide with the opponent, overwhelming him with momentum and power. If stopped, the Horse retreats, or feigns retreat, and attacks again from another angle.

Hawk

The Hawk is alert and watchful, its eyes penetrating the forest to seek its prey. The Hawk uses its agility and the ability to transform its body, shrinking and expanding as it moves around obstacles and penetrates into the heart of the forest. This transformative ability enables the Hawk to easily adapt to varied terrain and changing circumstances, allowing it to come out of nowhere when least expected. In combat, the Hawk spirals and overturns its body, shrinking and expanding, as it moves forward to enter the opponent's defenses.

Lion

The depiction of the Lion (*Shi*) in China resembles a kind of dog with a bear-like body. The Lion is often depicted with a ball. Like the Bear, the Lion uses shaking power, sometimes described as "shaking its fur." The Lion's body is pliable and agile. The Lion's movements are smooth, dynamic, and powerful, yet they also retain a playful quality. The Lion displays its flexible agility as it walks with an almost rolling gait, turns its body, and plays with a ball. In combat, the Lion is powerful and pliable, able to absorb and shake off attacks, and then enter the opponent's defenses.

**Renowned Master Sun Lu Tang
In the Lion Form**

Weapons Training in Ba Gua Zhang

Ba Gua Zhang training includes practice with traditional Chinese weapons, some of which are specific to the art of Ba Gua. Why train with traditional weapons? Some students resist weapons training because of the association of weapons with violence. Others complain that traditional weapons are not practical for modern self-defense. There is validity to these criticisms, but they are also a little simplistic. Weapon training is not only part of the culture of Chinese martial arts, but also part of the learning method.

Many Ba Gua teachers like Gao Ji Wu feel that weapon training hones *Shen Fa* ("Body Methods"), the techniques and methods of maneuvering the body. Weapons add another dimension to the basic body movements, by forcing the practitioner to accommodate and adapt to the shape, weight and intrinsic nature of the weapon. These adjustments strengthen the body, mind, intention and spirit.

The four classic Chinese weapons are the sword, saber, spear and staff. Although the sword and saber seem similar, they are in fact quite different, and each of these weapons requires specific energies, intention and body mechanics to wield it properly. The same is true of the two longer weapons spear and staff. These four weapons also provide the core movements and principles for understanding many of the other weapons.

Weapons extend out beyond the body's normal energy field and therefore require that we extend our intention and *Qi* outward, in order to interact with the various edges, points and surfaces of each weapon. The spear, in particular requires a fine-tuned intention that extends outward several feet to the tip of the spearhead. Weapons also have weight; so working with weapons increases functional strength. Working with weapons is like a form of mild weight training, however rather than isolating individual muscles or groups of muscles, the goal in working with weapons is to use the structure of the whole body to hold up and move the weapon. Each weapon develops different facets of functional strength. Weapons require us to understand how the momentum of the weapon influences our body movements. For example, the rooster knives are heavy and have many sharp edges. They must be held away from the body, and the practitioner must use circular steps and waist rotation in order to move the weapon properly. At the same time, "throwing" the weapon outward pulls the steps and aids waist rotation.

Traditional weapons teach tactics. Each weapon uses different techniques and therefore employs different tactics. For self-defense purposes, these techniques can easily be adapted to modern weapons or to improvised weapons. The different tactics learned through handling a weapon also trickle down to empty hand movements and impart deeper understanding of *Shen Fa*. Hence the saying: "use your hands like a sword and the sword like your hands." Training with weapons also teaches us to adapt the core movements of Ba Gua Zhang to different situations, so that the mind and body stay open and flexible.

Ba Gua Zhang weapons are often employed differently than weapons in other styles of martial arts. In Ba Gua Zhang, short weapons are used like long weapons, and long weapons from time to time are used like short weapons. Rather then wielding weapons with the arms and shoulders, the Ba Gua practitioner keeps the weapon relatively still, holding it up with the aligned structure of the body, while letting the steps and the body carry the weapon through space.

Ba Gua Saber (*Dao*)

The saber is a fearsome, powerful weapon that specializes in splitting, chopping, and slicing, intermixed with curved thrusts. To some degree, the saber is the quintessential Ba Gua weapon, because its curved shape interacts well with the curved, circular steps employed in Ba Gua. The saber has weight and cannot change direction quickly, so it stays relatively still while the body moves and changes. This creates an inherent deception. The saber seems to move, but in fact moves very little. The word *Dao* actually means "knife." The Ba Gua saber is not quite a sword and not quite a knife, so it employs the characteristic movements of both, seamlessly blending close-quarter movements and applications with more long-range movements and applications.

The back of the saber's blade is thick and can be used to deflect the opponent's attacks. Additionally, one can place one's left hand on the back of the saber to deliver a controlled, "two-handed" slice, or in preparation to reach out and control the opponent's weapon hand. The saber's handle is long allowing for an occasional shift to a powerful, two-handed chopping stroke.

One little-known benefit of the saber is that it trains movements in which one grasps the opponent's wrist in order to off-balance him or throw him, so to some degree, the Ba Gua saber is like a training partner.

Ba Gua Sword (*Jian*)

The *Jian* is a double-edged sword that is long and straight. It is often referred to as the "straight sword" in English. The *Jian* is lighter, quicker and more maneuverable then the saber, but not as sturdy. It can be compared to the Western rapier, whose movements influence modern epée play in sport fencing. The *Jian* cuts, slices and pierces with light plucking and "dotting" movements that are focused on the opponent's wrist and arm. Therefore, one generally avoids blade-to-blade contact with the opponent's weapon, except to lightly deflect, stick, adhere to, and control his or her sword. Hence, a high degree of skill is required to use the

Jian effectively. Master Zhao Da Yuan considers it the most difficult of the Ba Gua weapons

The use of the *Jian* is often compared to calligraphy, and the study of calligraphy is said to improve one's swordsmanship. For both of these reasons, the *Jian* is often considered to be considered the "gentleman's weapon," or an officer's weapon, in relation to the saber, which was a staple battlefield weapon. Some people say that the *Jian* is a more appropriate weapon for women because it relies less on ferocity and strength than does the saber. There may be some truth to this, but anyone who has seen Michelle Yeoh wield a saber in Kung Fu cinema, might beg to differ.

A little-known benefit of the *Jian* is that it trains movements in which one escapes from a wrist grab while simultaneously taking the initiative. Just like the saber, working with the *Jian* is like having a training partner.

Ba Gua Staff (*Gan*)

The Ba Gua Yin Yang Staff is a thick staff about six feet in length. The staff is a powerful weapon that can deliver bludgeoning blows or quick, deceptive thrusts. The staff mixes rotating, wrapping and enveloping movements with strikes and thrusts. Its weight and length require that the practitioner use fluid body actions to generate these movements. The staff, like all of the two-handed weapons, teaches the practitioner to connect both sides of the body, as the two sides are effectively chained together through the connection of the hands to the staff. In order to freely strike with either end of the staff, one's footwork and handwork must seamlessly link. This has many parallels with the hand forms and with the connection of intention, *Qi* and power. The pushing, pulling and sliding movements of staff also trains many of the power dynamics involved in throwing techniques.

Seven Star Stick (*Qi Xing Gun*)

The Seven Star Stick is also called the Whip Stick (*Bian Gun*), or Heart High Stick (*Xin Gun*). It is essentially a walking stick, used for centuries by Chinese people in the countryside as both an essential tool and a weapon of self-defense. The Seven Star Stick is lighter and faster than the Ba Gua Staff. It is a highly flexible and adaptable weapon with many modes of use. Because it can be used one-handed or two-handed, the Seven Star Stick includes movements of the Staff, Spear, Sword and Saber, as well as its own unique movements, blending them all together in a series of high speed changes. Actions of the Seven Star Stick also include locks and throws, as well as counters to grabs. Like the staff, the Seven Star Stick challenges one's ability to tightly link hand and body changes with footwork.

Ba Gua Cane (*Zhang*)

When Ba Gua practitioners like Gao Yi Sheng and Liu Feng Zhai moved from the countryside to the city, they adapted the actions of the walking stick to the city version of a walking stick, the cane. The cane is often constructed from a flexible but sturdy wood like rattan. The Ba Gua Cane, like the Seven Star Stick, blends actions of the Staff, Spear, Sword and Saber together in rapid-fire sequences that exemplify the art of constant change. However, the crooked end of the cane adds another dimension: hooking, locking and throwing the opponent. The crook can be used to devastating effect when hooking limbs and even the neck. Because a wooden cane can be carried anywhere, it is very practical for self-defense.

Spear (*Qiang*)

The spear is considered by many to be one of the most difficult weapons in the Chinese martial arts. This is partially because when using the spear, energy and intention must be extended outward to the tip of the spear as it rotates, cuts and pierces with precision and refined power. The Chinese spear is long (6.5 to 7.5 feet), and has a tapered and flexible shaft with a crest of red horsehair behind the tip. The movement of the horsehair as the spear, thrusts, circles and rotates distracts the opponent. In training, these same movements provide feedback relating to correct rotation and power delivery. Another difficult, yet valuable educational aspect of the spear is that very small movements in the hands and body produce much larger movements at the tip of the weapon. The spear therefore refines one's internal control of exterior movement to a high level.

The flexible shaft of the spear helps to develop a refined, elastic, shaking power in the empty hand forms. At the same time, this elastic power is part of the technique of using the spear to deflect and attack.

Ba Gua Rooster Claw Yin Yang Knives (*Ba Gua Ji Zhao Yin Yang Rui*)

There are many multi-edged, hooked knife-like weapons that are used in pairs in Ba Gua Zhang. This is partly because the footwork of Ba Gua lends itself to knife-like weapons, but also because there is disagreement about the nature of the Founder's (Dong Hai Chuan) personal weapon. Some say that this weapon looked like the Rooster Claw Knives pictured below, others argue that it resembled the Mandarin Duck Knives (which themselves have many variations and names).

The Rooster Claw Knife is a unique weapon that lies along the forearm, but can suddenly be extended outward to increase its length when chopping and hooking. Parts of the Rooster Claw Knife resemble the tail and head of the rooster, and it also has a distinctive claw from which it derives it name.

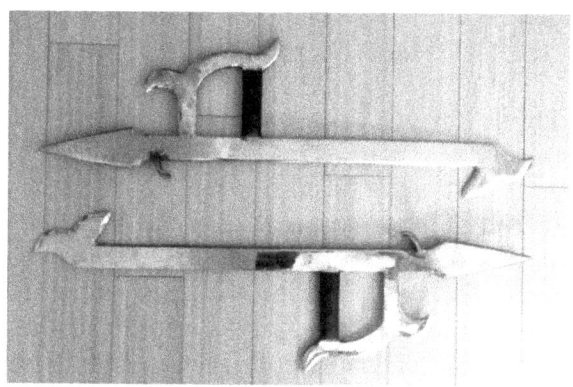

Ba Gua Hook Sickle Swords (*Ba Gua Gou Lian Jian*)

The Ba Gua Hook Sickle Swords resemble a kind of tomahawk more than a sword. In usage they resemble the Rooster Claw Knives, and in fact many of the movements for these two weapons are essentially the same. The difference is in the *Shen Fa* and power dynamic. The Rooster Claw Knives focus their action on the back, and the shoulder girdle, with power and *Jin* manifesting in the upper arm and elbow. The Hook Sickle Swords focus more on the shoulder, elbow and wrist, with power manifesting in the forearm and wrist.

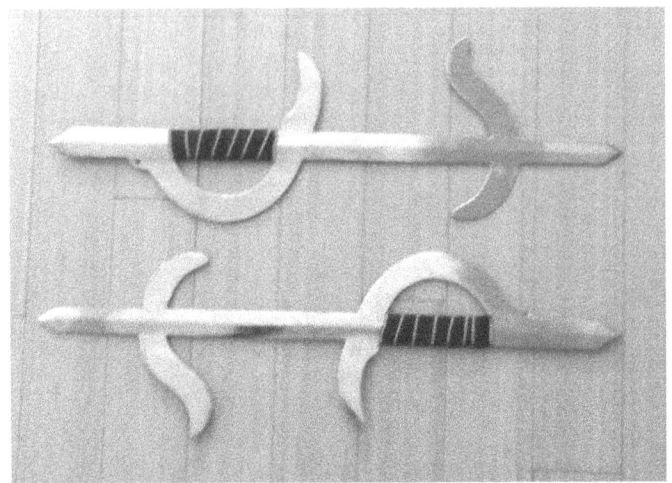

Hook Sickle Swords

Mandarin Duck Knives (*Yuan Yang Pu*)

Yuan Yang Pu can also be translated as "Mandarin Duck Axes." In different styles of Ba Gua Zhang The Mandarin Duck Knives have different names (Deer Horn Knives, Sun Moon Knives, etc.), variations in design, and therefore usage. The Mandarin Duck Knives pierce, chop, hook, lift up, press down, deflect, and cut. The crescent moon part of the weapon can be used to trap and deflect, and the tips of the "moon" can also rake and pierce. In training, the weapon develops subtle body changes, in conjunction with deft elbow and wrist movements. This weapon is sometimes referred to as the Yin Yang Knives, because it combines a Yang (straight) aspect with a Yin (curved) aspect.

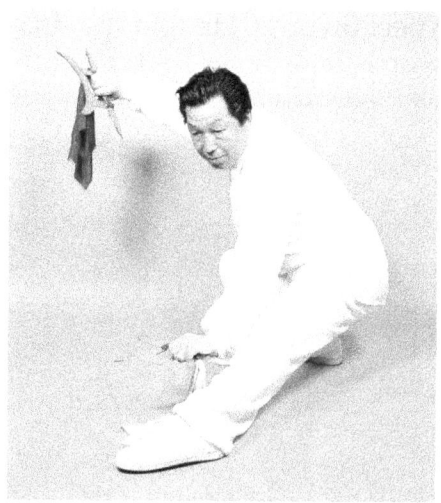

Master Gao Ji Wu with the Mandarin Duck Knives

A Pair of Mandarin Duck Knives

Ba Gua Wind Wheel Swords (*Ba Gua Feng Lun Jian*)

The Wind-Wheel Swords are a unique pair of weapons that move in unexpected circles and arcs, while deflecting, looping, hooking, piercing, and slicing. This weapon was a favorite of Li Zi Ming and Wang Shi Tong. Wang Shi Tong taught me the Wind Wheel Sword form and gave me his pair of Wind Wheel Swords. He told me that historically the Wind-Wheel Swords had never been used in actual combat, but that they were very useful for training *Shen Fa.*

Master Li Zi Ming Wielding the Wind Wheel Swords
(Courtesy Martial arts of China Magazine)

Ba Gua Elbow Knives (*Ba Gua Zhou Dao*)

The Rooster Claw Knives are sometimes referred to as Elbow Knives, because they lay along the forearm. However, in Liang Style Ba Gua, Elbow Knives refer to a pair of long knives, like the American Bowie knife, that have a slightly a curved blade. The Elbow Knives may also have a clipped point with a "false edge." There are no specific forms with these weapons. Students learn to interpret Ba Gua's empty-hand forms, particularly forms that focus on the use of the

142

elbow, like the Thirteen Elbows, and translate them to this weapon.

Ba Gua Point Striking Stick (*Ba Gua Dian Xue Gun*)

The Ba Gua Point Striking Stick is a modern adaptation of a Xing Yi and Ba Gua weapons called respectively the "iron finger" and "judge's pen." These metal weapons had either points or barbs and could be concealed in the hand or in the sleeve. As a self-defense weapon, the iron finger and judge's pen were used to surprise the opponent and amplify one's force in striking vital points, increase leverage when locking joints and aid in blocking and deflecting. The modern Point Striking Stick is made of wood, tapers at one end, has a knob on the other end, and a leather or cloth loop that one slips over the middle finger, so that the hand can open without dropping the weapon. It is hidden when the hand is open. This weapon is useful for chopping, piercing, and locking. The Point Striking Stick is particularly useful as a force equalizer in self-defense situations.

The Strategy and Spirit of Ba Gua Zhang as a Martial Art

The strategy and spirit of Ba Gua Zhang as a martial art is very much in tune with Daoist notions of non-action (*Wu Wei*), and the nature of change and transformation. New York Internal Art Instructor Eric Darton explains this as follows:

The first and most (retroactively) shocking realization, taught by the continuous chain-linking movements of the form itself, is that there is nothing in the practice that supports the idea of a beginning or an end. There are no "goals," only cyclical potentiation of movement, actualization and resorption. One does not seek to strike a particular blow, though that blow may happen. One does not maneuver an opponent in order to execute, say, a joint lock, or a throw. Rather it is the interplay of your and your opponent's movements that creates the "space" for the lock or throw to occur. If a dispositive move happens, it often comes quite unexpectedly out of the build-up of circumstances. The practitioner trained in this form thus has no formula for what she or he will do in a given situation – the situation creates opportunities to draw the opponent into an unsustainable position. In short, I do not try to defeat my opponent. Instead, by maintaining the integrity of my structure, I facilitate the conditions for his self-defeat.[50]

---

[50] *Writing, Politics and the Internal Art of Ba Gua Zhang: Further Notes Toward a Dao of Writing,* by Eric Darton, 2015.

BA GUA ZHANG AS A PSYCHO-SPIRITUAL PATH

Although Ba Gua Zhang is a martial art, for many practitioners its most important facet is the ability of Ba Gua Zhang to promote health and deeper engagement with the world. In this sense, Ba Gua Zhang provides a template for integrating body, mind and spirit. The foundation of psycho-spiritual health is physical and mental health. Ba Gua Zhang's emphasis on creating internal harmony and balance, self-cultivation of mind and body, and adapting to change help one to more easily negotiate life and interactions with others. Ba Gua's martial tactic of changing with the changing circumstances, or, as some people say, "going with the flow," helps us to understand and adapt to the natural world, and its manifestations within us. The seasons, weather, the harmony and majesty of nature with its cycles of growth, flourishing, decay, and renewal affect us and move through us. Understanding change also helps us understand how to have a healthy relationship with ourselves and with others, so that we can adapt to different situations and cultures.

Embodied Spirituality

It is one thing to study and appreciate Chinese philosophy and its approach to harmony with nature intellectually. It is another to actually embody these ideas on both a conscious and subconscious level. The practice of Ba Gua Zhang, through movement and mind-intention, allows you to deeply experience and appreciate the natural forces that not only act upon us from moment to moment, but that make us human. Ba Gua trains you to sense, express and exploit the universal energies of forces expressed symbolically by the Eight Trigrams: Heaven, Earth, Fire, Water, Wind/Wood, Lake, Mountain, and Thunder. These eight forces are eight expressions of the *Qi* that move through the outside world and also move within us. Heaven, in this sense, has nothing to due with the Judeo-Christian notion of an afterlife, but rather represents the cosmic forces that influence our life on Earth. Practicing Ba Gua Zhang attunes your inner landscape to the outer landscape and the universal flow of *Qi*, so that you can move in harmony with the world and all of its manifestations, transformations and changes.

In Daoist thought, the inner landscape of the body is a microcosm of the cosmic forces in the macrocosm. The mind and spirit can tap into and work with the universal energies of the macrocosm so that ultimately one vibrates in harmony with these energies. Ba Gua Zhang is a method of actualizing this resonance, using the *Yi Jing* as a guide to aid practitioners in exploring and connecting to the eight universal energies that exist inside and outside the body. Exploring these energies deep within, while simultaneously sensing them in the surrounding world, forges a connection between the individual and the cosmos, allowing an understanding of universal truths that are not graspable by language and intellect alone. Circle Walking Nei Gong and the Single and Double Palm Changes are key practices that allow one to develop and actualize this deep connection. The practice of Ba Gua Zhang imparts the potential for the mind and spirit to reach beyond the limitations of the body, and connect with the universal and numinous forces of change and transformation.

The Daoist Zhuang Zi (Chuang Tzu) describes this numinous state as a kind of flowing or adaptive cognition, as opposed to a fixed cognition. The clarity of mind that is fostered through the practice of Ba Gua, when applied to everyday life, allows us to make more precise and less biased decisions and perceptions, so that the mind is less likely to be fooled by circumstances, people and delusional thinking. By re-connecting to the "Original Breath" through practices like Circle Walking Nei Gong, one slowly returns to the "Original Mind," an inner knowing, or inner wisdom, that is outside of analytical thinking mechanisms.

The spirituality espoused in Daoist-influenced arts like Ba Gua is not viewed as transcendent (outside of us and the world we live in), but as immanent (within the world and us), connecting us to a power or force that infuses all of our being from moment to moment. It can be tapped into by direct practices such as sitting or moving meditation.[51]

Balancing Yin and Yang

The practice of circle walking balances Yin and Yang. This balance occurs in many ways. Three ways that Yin and Yang interact in Circle Walking Nei Gong are of particular interest. First, walking in a circle requires the alternation of two different steps. The outside foot (Yang Foot) makes a *Koubu* (hook step), and the inside foot (Yin Foot) makes a *Baibu* (swing step or pendulum step). The inside foot goes straight, and the outside foot moves in a hooked curve. The Yang Foot closes inward toward the Yin, and the Yin Step goes forward toward the periphery of the circle (toward the Yang) This mode of stepping creates an alternation of opening and closing, and allows Yin and Yang to interchange. Secondly, as you walk you are sensing the interchange of Yin and Yang that occurs as each step changes from a Yin Step to a Yang Step and back again. For example, just as one leg becomes Yang, taking all the body weight and driving the body forward, it is already beginning its transformation to Yin. The shift from Yin to Yang and Yang to Yin is very subtle. Circle walking using the Mud

---

[51] *Early Taoist Contemplation and Its Resonance in the American Academy:* An Interview with Harold Roth. http://www.holosforum.org/halroth.html

Wading Step fine-tunes one's sense of when weight and power shift from one leg to the other, creating spiral Yin and Yang forces between the feet that are transmitted upward through the body. Lastly, walking clockwise is Yang and walking counter-clockwise is Yin. Each direction stimulates the brain and body in different ways. Walking in both directions balances the two sides of the brain and balances the muscles on the inside and outside of the legs, and on the two sides of the torso. This in turn balances the three Yang meridians on the outside of the legs with the three Yin Meridians on the inside of the legs.

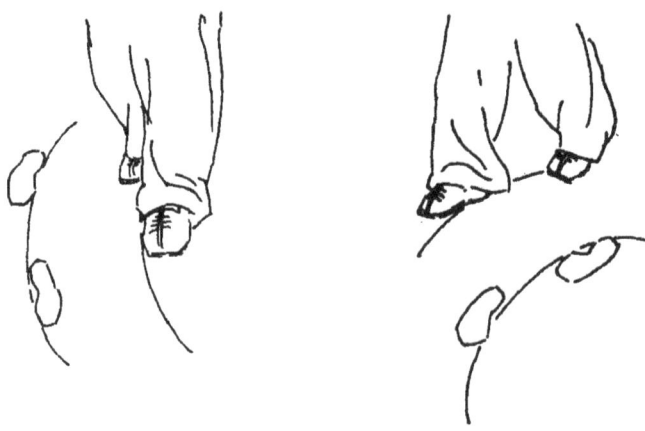

Walking the Circle

Changing direction on the circle works with the balanced and smooth interchange between Yin and Yang in yet another way. The body turns in on itself and then opens outward, creating an internal figure-8 that resembles the Tai Ji Diagram with its graphic interweaving and inter-transformation of Yin and Yang. Even the two seminal methods of changing palms and directions can be said to be relatively Yin and Yang. The Single Palm Change is more

Yang, and the Double Palm Change more Yin. Therefore, the practice of circling and changing directions further harmonizes the shifts between Yin and Yang, which in turn balances and harmonizes the body on many levels.

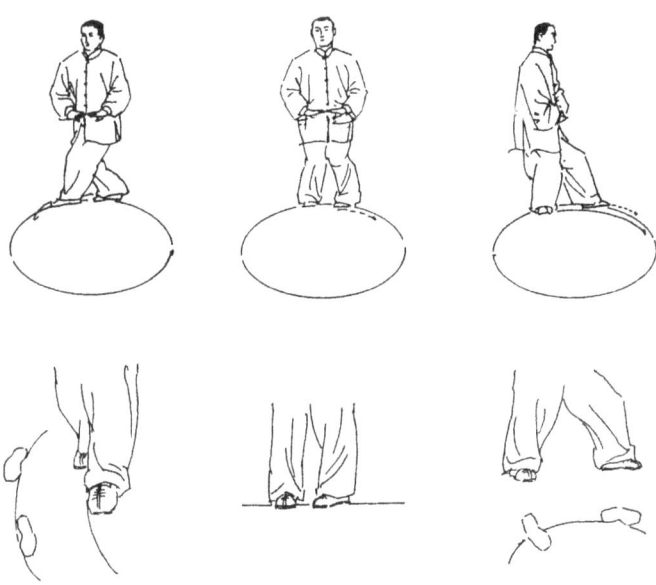

Changing Directions on the Circle

As you walk using *Koubu* and *Baibu* steps, the legs pass close together so that the ankles and thighs almost brush each other. This action is sometimes called "scissor legs." This stepping pattern squeezes the thighs together, activating the sexual energy and strengthening the reproductive system and Kidneys, which are the foundation of the body's energy. As the foot lands, the *Yongquan* ("Bubbling Well") acu-point on the bottom of the foot is stimulated, which activates the Kidney meridian and its connections to *Dantian* and *Mingmen*. Every step creates a pumping action in *Yongquan* that is transmitted upward to fill and strengthen the Kidney energy.

In Ba Gua Zhang's seminal movement, the Single Palm Change, the body internally and externally actualizes the Tai Ji diagram and the Ba Gua. The Single Palm Change recreates the model of the universe inside the body, and further balances the Yin and Yang forces inside of us in a profound and powerful way, while simultaneously connecting these internal expressions of Heaven and Earth to the macrocosm around us.

Ba Gua -Tai Ji Diagram

After circling and changing for a period of time, one ends by standing still and sensing inside the body. At this moment many practitioners experience a sense of connection with the cosmos. One feels not only the turning within, but also the turning of the earth and the planets. My own experience of this is when standing still, it is difficult to tell if you are turning, or if everything around you is slowly turning, and you feel the force of that turning creating spirals inside of you.

The Human Body as a Numinous Vessel

In Chinese medicine and Daoist thinking, our energetic being stems from the sexual energy, which is the physical embodiment of creation within us, represented by *Jing* (Essence). In some sense *Jing* is our connection to the Earth, to the past, to our genetic potential. *Jing* forms the foundation of the body's power and energy, the *Qi*. In a psycho-spiritual sense, *Qi* is our embodied energy and our connection to the world, and the processes, which sustain our life, here and now. *Shen* (Spirit) is replenished through the interaction of *Jing* and *Qi* and the transformative action of the *Qi*. *Shen* allows us to look above and beyond ourselves. *Shen* connects us both to what is transcendent within us, and to the transcendent that lies outside of ourselves.

We connect to Heaven through the *Baihui* ("Hundred Meeting") acu-point on the top of the head. We connect to Earth through the *Yongquan* acu-points on the bottoms of our feet. Our vital force circulates upward from Earth to Heaven, and downward from Heaven to Earth. Our physical body, and our *Qi*, consciousness, and spirit act as the pivot connecting these two energies.

The three aspects of our being, *Jing, Qi* and *Shen* are intimately connected. We need the driving force of our sexual energy and the past to move ahead and fully experience life in the here and now. And we need to communicate with what is beyond us for our life to grow and flourish. If we lose our connection with what is beyond, our connection to our creativity, wisdom and vision, then to some degree we shut down as human beings. We close down to life and operate only at the level of survival and procreation, losing the connection to our higher self. However, if the pathways between these three aspects of our being stay open, we can live and evolve with grace and harmony.

151

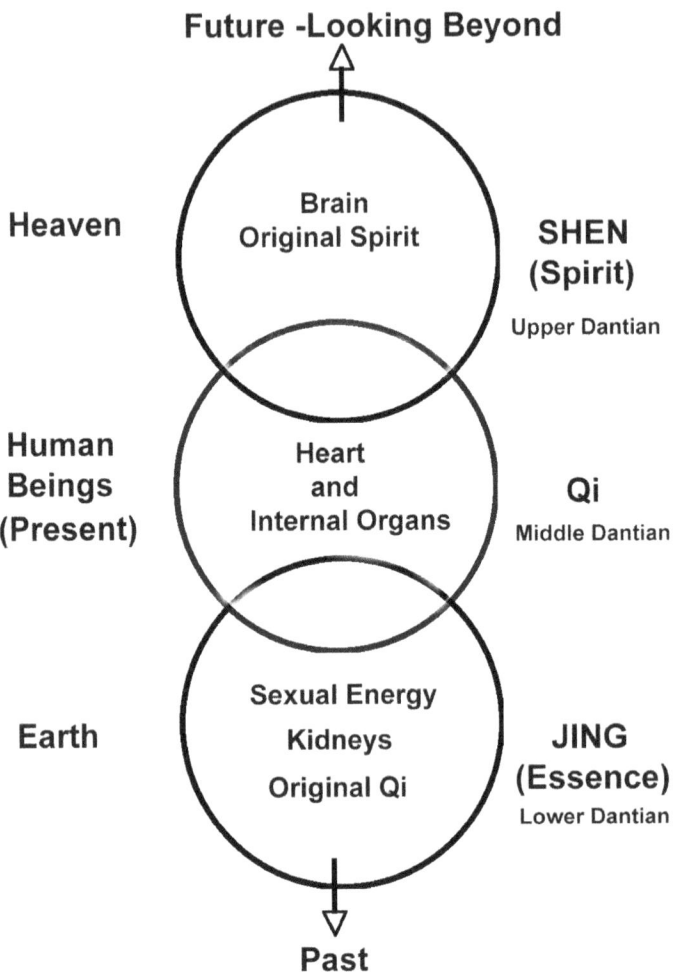

The Revitalizing Power of Circle Walking

One way we can recharge this system is simply by walking. Walking and particularly Circle Walking with alignment and focused Mind-Intention stimulates the "Bubbling Well" (*Yongquan*) acu-points on the bottoms of the feet, connecting the energies of Earth, Human Beings and Heaven in a single step. A single step of aligned Circle Walking jump-starts a process that revitalizes our Kidneys, replenishes *Jing* and activates the *Qi,* so that transformation can unfold harmoniously and engender a clear and present *Shen.*

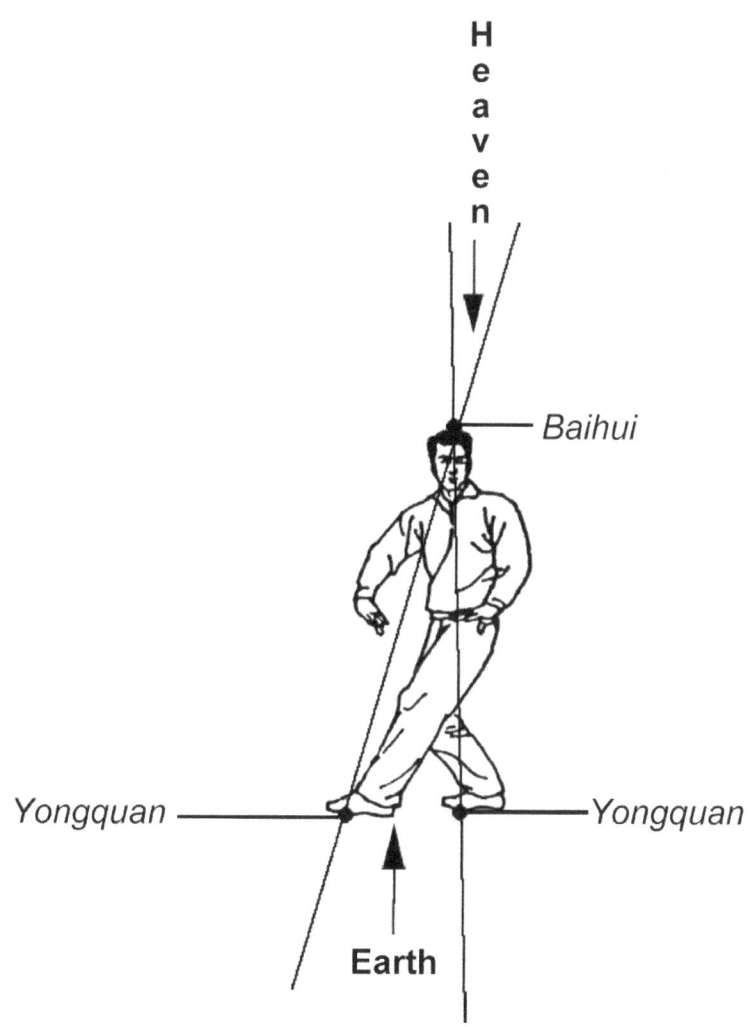

By walking the circle, we move forward through life, but at the same time with each circle we return to the beginning. This combination of forward movement, combined with the energetic spirals that both enfold inward and expand outward as the steps change, reinvigorates the body and re-incites one's life with every step. To some degree, the power of walking the circle lies in it continuity, its cyclical revolutions that have no beginning or end. Each circle builds on the last, arousing the body's vital forces so that they exponentially gather and coalesce, continuously tapping an inexhaustible potential for transformation and change. With every step around the circle, Ba Gua Zhang, the art of walking par excellence, offers us a unique opportunity to fully engage with our lives and with the world around us.

OVERVIEW OF THE BA GUA ZHANG CURRICULUM

Foundational Level

Yin Yang Patting Nei Gong (*Ba Gua Yin Yang Pai Da Nei Gong)*

Dao Yin Health Preservation Exercises (*Dao Yin Yang Sheng*)

Nine Palace Dao Yin (*Ju Gong Dao Yin*)

28 Foundational Exercises (*Ba Gua Ji Ben Gong*)

Basic Standing Meditation or Post Standing (*Zhan Zhuang*)

12 Ba Gua Standing Postures (*Ba Gua Shi Er Zhan Zhuang*)

Qi Cultivation Exercises (*Qi Ji Gong*)

Ba Gua Circle Walking Nei Gong (*Ding Shi Ba Gua Zhang*)

Foundational Partner Exercises (*Dui Lian Ji Ben Gong*)

Single Palm Change (*Dan Huan Zhang*)

Double Palm Change (*Shuang Huan Zhang*)

Intermediate Level

Tian Gan (Heavenly Stem) Exercises (*Tian Gan Nei Gong*)

Single Palm Change (*Dan Huan Zhang*)

Ba Gua Curriculum Overview

Double Palm Change (*Shuang Huan Zhan*)

Old Eight Palms (*Lao Ba Zhang*)

Eight Hands (*Ba Zhang*)

Eight Elbows Form (*Ba Zhou*)

Single Movement Practice (*Dan Dong Lian Xi*)

Basic Throwing Methods (*Shuai Fa*)

Qin Na Locking and Capturing Skills (*Na Fa*)

Kicking Developmental Exercises (*Ti Fa Ji Ben Gong*)

Kicking Drills and Techniques (*Ti Fa*)

Bone Breathing (*Xi Hu Gu*)

Marrow Washing Nei Gong (*Xi Sui Jing*)

Ba Gua Saber Foundational Practice (*Ba Gua Dao Ji Ben Gong*)

Ba Gua Staff Foundational Practice (*Ba Gua Gun Ji Ben Gong*)

Advanced Level

Basic Seated Meditation (*Jing Gong*)

Golden Fluid Returning to Dantian Meditation (*Jin Ye Hai Dan Tian Gong*)

13 Elbows Form (*Shi San Zhou*)

64 Hands (*Liu Shi Si Zhi Tang*)

72 Techniques (*Qi Shi Er Zhao*)

Ba Gua Chain Linking Form (*Lian Huan Ba Gua Zhang*)

Eight Animal Ba Gua (*Xian Tian Xiang Xing Zhang*)

Changing Palms (*Ba Gua Hua Huan Zhang*)

Eight Direction Palm (*Ba Mian Zhang*)

Weapons

  Single weapons

- Saber (*Ba Gua Dao*)

- Sword (*Ba Gua Jian*)

- Staff (*Ba Gua Gan*)

- Seven Star Stick (*Qi Xing Gun*)

- Ba Gua Cane (*Ba Gua Zhang*)

- Spear (*Qiang*)

- Ba Gua Point Striking Stick (*Ba Gua Dian Xue Gun*)

Paired Weapons

- Rooster Claw Knives (*Ba Gua Ji Zhao Yin Yang Rui*)

- Mandarin Duck Knives (*Yuan Yang Pu*)

- Hook Sickle Swords (*Ba Gua Gou Lian Jian*)

- Wind Wheel Swords (*Ba Gua Feng Lun Jian*)

- Ba Gua Elbow Knives (*Ba Gua Zhou Dao*)

A Medical and Physiological Study of the Health-Giving Effects of Ba Gua Zhang Practice

By Kang Ge Wu

Beijing Physical Culture Institute)[52]

Ba Gua Zhang (Eight Diagram Palm) is a *Wushu* form with a relatively short history. Apart from its combative value, it has proved to be an effective means of preventing disease and promoting health and longevity. For this reason, it has gained widespread popularity among the Chinese people.

In order to make a medical and physiological study of the health-giving effects of Ba Gua Zhang, a comprehensive research group was formed by 13 members of the teaching groups of Sports Physiology, Wushu, Sports Medicine and Anatomy at the Beijing Physical Culture Institute. Their research program involved 60 males ranging from 60 to 82 years of age who were divided into two groups: (1) the exercise group of 30 persons who practice Ba Gua Zhang regularly; and (2) the control group consisting of 30 healthy retired workers. They were given X-ray photographic examinations of the chest, waist and hips, as well as a number of medical physiological tests consisting of items

---

[52] *A Medical and Physiological Study of the Health Giving Effects of Ba Gua Zhang Practice* by Kang Ge Wu, (Published n Martial arts of China Magazine Vol. 1, No. 4 1990. China Direct publishing San Francisco) p.153-4.

such as range of movement of the spine and hip joints, breathing function, circulation function, the work capacity of muscles, eyesight, hearing, balancing ability, and circumferences of the limbs. Statistical treatments with BCM II type electronic computer of the data obtained showed clearly that the exercise group is better than the control group in all respects. This amply proves that regular practice of Ba Gua Zhang can promote health and slow down retrograde changes related to senility.

1. Improving Structures and Functions of the Locomotive Organs

The basic Ba Gua Zhang movements consist of walking around in circles. By doing so, the limbs are subjected to continuous exercise in extension and flexion, adduction and abduction, which helps improve and maintain the range of the joint movements. Movements of the joints over a large range of motion and in various directions within the anatomical limits causes repeated stretches on the distal points of the corresponding muscle groups on the bone surfaces and around the joints. They also speed up substance metabolism, activate the osteoblasts, improve blood supply to the bones and promote adaptive changes of bone structure. The following comparisons were made between the exercise and control groups in the range of movement of the waist, lateral bends of the torso, rotation of the hip joints, and forward bend of the torso (all figures denote average values).

Activity	Exercise Group	Control Group
1. Waist Turn (legs in fixed position)		
Leftward		
	102.87°	58.31°
Rightward		
	102.97°	53.62°

Activity	Exercise Group	Control Group

2. Lateral Bend of Torso

(Knees held stiff)

Leftward

	35.63°	25°

Rightward

	36.12°	28.52°

3. External Rotation of Hip Joints

(Knees held stiff)

   Right Thigh

	56.63°	45.10°

  Left Thigh

	57.68°	46.17°

4. Forward Bend if Torso (knees held stiff)

6.70 cm	-6.83cm*

*The minus sign means that the subjects in the control group failed to touch the stool on which they were standing in the forward bending test, their fingertips coming no further down than 6.83 cm above the surface of the stool.

The above table shows that the exercise group is superior to the control group in all the items tested. With most old people, the range of joint movement markedly decreases with age. It is believed that this decreases elasticity in the muscles and muscle tendons, proliferation of the connective tissue in the muscles, etc. and may also affect the movement of the spine. The fact that the range of joint movement displayed by the exercise group had been found to be clearly superior to that of the control group is ample proof of the benefits derived from long years of Ba Gua Zhang practice.

Age-related retrograde changes of the skeletal system are usually indicated by such symptoms as osteophyma (hyperosteogeny in the pre-vertebral part), osteoporosis in the pyramid, abnormality of the weight-bearing line in the acetabulum and abnormality of the caput femoris (deformity of the caput femoris, osteoporosis, osteophyma formation, etc). Osteophyma results from the degeneration of the intervertebral disc and the abnormal activity of the pyramid, which cause consistent over-stretch of the ligaments around the pyramid (the anterior and posterior longitudinal ligaments) and irritate the periosteum to which the ligaments are attached.

Osteoporosis in the pyramid manifests itself in such symptoms as thinning of the bone cortex, rarefaction and thinning of the bony trabecula, and the decrease of bone density. All these lead to deformation and inflexibility of the joints. The change of the radian in the weight bearing line of the hip joint means there is deformity of the joint surface and may to a certain extent affect or damage the function of the joints. From the frontal and lateral X-ray photographs of the waists and hips of the subjects in the two groups, the average number of Osteophyma in the lumbar vertebrae has been found to be 12.174 in the exercise group and 16.857 in the control group. Osteoporosis in the lumbar vertebrae affects 17.8% of the persons in the exercise group, while the figure in the control group is as high as 49.3%. It is also noted that the transverse diameter of the femur (averaging 34.98 mm) and the thickness of the bone cortex (19.87 mm) in the exercise group are obviously better than the corresponding measurements taken of the control group (32.06 mm and 17.47 mm respectively). Osteoporosis of the femur and rarefaction of the bony trabecula affect only 40% of the persons in the exercise group, but no less than 60% of those in the control group. All this shows that regular practice of Ba Gua Zhang can help density of the bone substance and thicken the bones, thus strengthening their resistance to breaks, bends, compressions and twists. Ba Gua

Zhang exercises can also help enlarge limb circumferences and build muscular strength, as evidenced by a comparison of measurements taken of the two groups:

Item	Exercise Group	Control Group
Circumference of Chest		
	93.67 cm	86.78 cm
Right Upper Arm (Relaxed)		
	27.63 cm	24.98 cm
Right Thigh		
	54.42 cm	47.67 cm
Right Shank		
	35.61 cm	32.97 cm
Grip Strength		
Right Hand		
	28.40 kg	21.27 kg
Left Hand		
	24.87 kg	20.20 kg
Twisting Strength		
Forearm Rotating Outward		
Right Arm		
	14.71 kg	10.45 kg
Left Arm		
	13.80 kg	10.65 kg
12 Minute Run (or walk-run)		
	1158.97 m	1002.49 m

2. Strengthening the Respiratory Function

When practicing Ba Gua Zhang, one is required to sink one's *Qi* down to *Dantian* (elixir field), a region below the navel where breaths are stored and released in respiration. Breathing is of the abdominal type, and should be even, soft and deep. This way of breathing helps enlarge the motor range of the diaphragm and thorax, thus strengthening the respiratory function. The following table of comparative figures obtained from our tests shows that Ba Gua Zhang exercises induce stronger respiratory functions:

Item	Exercise Group	Control Group
Chest Circumference Difference Between Inhalation & Exhalation	4.95 cm	3.30 cm
Vital Capacity	2285.78 ml	1713.97 ml
Max. Ventilation Volume	44.06 liters	30.49 liters

3. Improving the Function of the Cardiovascular System

In practicing Ba Gua Zhang, the expansion and contraction of the skeletal muscles, the movement of the joints, and the constant change of the abdominal pressure brought about by rhythmic abdominal respiration, all contribute to the acceleration of the venous backflow. Moreover, many more capillaries are open during exercise, thus decreasing the peripheral resistance of the minor blood vessels. All this helps improve blood circulation of the blood and the nourishment of the cardiac muscle, thus resulting in a better function of the cardiovascular system.

Electrocardiographic tests have detected abnormal ECG in 41.38% of the subjects in the exercise group and 65.520% of those in the control group. It has been reported that the abnormal ECG detectable rate for old people is 67.60%. By comparison, the rate of normal ECG in the exercise group is higher than that in the control group. The difference should be credited to the salubrious effects of Ba Gua Zhang.

4. Improving the Function of the Nervous System

Ba Gua Zhang practice requires great concentration. Practitioners at a more advanced stage are even required to cultivate a sense of real fighting and an ability to apply their combative techniques according to changing circumstances. Exercising in this manner can help improve the flexibility of the nervous system. Besides, a Ba Gua Zhang performer has to walk round and round in circles, turning now to the right and now to the left as he changes his hand movements. In this way he keeps rotating his body on its vertical axis, which helps improve the function of the vestibular analyzer.

Reaction time is usually used as an index for testing the flexibility of the nervous system. In recent years, the electromechanical delay index has come into frequent use. Reaction time refers to the interval of time between the appearance of a signal and the occurrence of myo-electric reaction. Its length depends on the excitatory state of the central nervous system and the flexibility of the nervous process. Electromechanical delay refers to the interval of time between the occurrence of electric currents produced by muscular contraction and the appearance of mechanical reaction. Its length has much to do with the speed of muscular contraction. Tests have shown the differences between the exercise and control groups in reaction time and electromechanical delay

Item	Exercise Group	Control Group
Reaction Time		
	198.02 millisec.	230.4 millisec.
Electro-mechanical Delay		
	64.19 millisec.	77.96 millisec.

With a home-made LX-type electronic balancing apparatus, experiments have been conducted on the two groups of old people to test their balancing ability while standing on both feet with their eyes open or closed, in each case for 30 seconds. The average degrees of their bodies' deviation from the vertical were measured and the figures are given below:

Item	Exercise Group	Control Group
Deviation with Eyes Open		
	7.65°	9.14°
Deviation with Eyes Closed		
	8.13°	11.15°

The degree of deviation displayed by the exercise group is smaller than that shown by the control group, especially when the eyes are closed. With the eyes closed, the use of vision for body balance is precluded so that the test concentrates on the function of the vestibular and muscular senses. The above-mentioned results of the test prove the beneficial effects of Ba Gua Zhang practice on the nervous system.

Lightning Source UK Ltd.
Milton Keynes UK
UKHW020634220921
391008UK00012B/673